THE PACIFIC
IN THE 1990s

Economic and Strategic Change

Janos Radvanyi

UNIVERSITY
PRESS OF
AMERICA

Lanham • New York • London

*Center for International Security
and Strategic Studies*

√330.99
R119p

Co-Published by arrangement with the Center for
International Security and Strategic Studies

Library of Congress Cataloging-in-Publication Data

The Pacific in the 1990s : economic and strategic change / edited
by Janos Radvanyi.
p.   cm.
Includes bibliographical references and index.
1. Economic forecasting—Pacific Area.   2. Pacific Area—Economic
conditions.   3. United States—Military policy—Forecasting.
4. Pacific Area—Military policy—Forecasting.
I. Radványi, János.
HC681.P289   1990   330.99—dc20   90–12793 CIP

ISBN 0–8191–7900–0 (alk. paper)
ISBN 0–8191–7901–9 (pbk. : alk. paper)

 The paper used in this publication meets the minimum requirements of
American National Standard for Information Sciences—Permanence
of Paper for Printed Library Materials, ANSI Z39.48–1984.

Table of Contents

Preface

Our anthology differs from most other published books and commentaries in several respects. First, it not only focuses on the usual geopolitical issues and power balances, but it also concentrates heavily on the complex interactions between social, political, and economic forces and changing security postures in the Asian Pacific and the world. Second, it offers a detailed and unique projection of relations between the world's two greatest economic powers, the United States and Japan, and the world's most populous country, China. Third, it shows how the startling rise of four newly industrialized countries in the area—Taiwan, Singapore, South Korea, and Hong Kong—will be a determining factor in Asian Pacific fortunes in the next decade.

No defense-related study would be complete without evaluation of the "new thinking" of Soviet General Secretary Mikhail Gorbachev. Gorbachev's approach to safeguarding Soviet interests in the Far East clearly differs from the confrontational style of his predecessors; what is more, the recent easing of Sino-Soviet border tensions and the withdrawal of Soviet troops from Afghanistan are positive signs that the Soviet leader's declarations of intent are followed by action. Recently, all countries in the Pacific Basin recognize that the dramatic reforms occurring in Eastern Europe and the shift from communist party rule to presidential power in the Soviet Union have altered the strategic scene. Yet, Soviet occupation of Japan's northern territories still hampers Soviet-Japanese relations, and the Soviets' continued failure to cooperate in the lessening of tensions in this regard gives cause for skepticism about their long-term plans for the region. Also, Japan's suspicion of Mikhail Gorbachev's doctrine of "reasonable sufficiency" for the Soviet forces in Asia is fueled by the fact that between a quarter and a third of the Red army today is stationed in the Soviet Far East, mostly on Sakhalin Island and the Kamchatka peninsula. One third of the Soviet strategic missiles, 2,400 combat aircraft, 100 warships, 160 submarines and 600,000 soldiers are deployed there. On top of that, M124 attack helicopters and three armored divisions are stationed within invasion distance of Japan. In spite of this negative attitude of the Kremlin, the Japanese—as it is pointed out in the anthology—hope to resolve the territorial problem and eventually to conclude a peace treaty with the Soviet Union. But, right now, the cold war between Japan and Russia is still on.

Several of the chapters in this book have become especially significant in the wake of news from Beijing's Tiananmen Square on the night of June 3, 1989. Since that date, the world has watched closely to see to what degree China will revert to doctrinaire Marxism and to gauge how current changes might affect reforms within the country as well as China's relations with the West. This collection stresses repeatedly, and from many points of view, the importance of a continuing U.S.-Chinese relationship, including special military ties. We see more and more evidence that the governments on both sides still agree on this point, despite the differences which surfaced in June. To cite but one example, Washington is still receiving data on Soviet nuclear and missile tests and other seismic disturbances from U.S. monitoring stations in China's western provinces, and these stations are still serviced by Chinese personnel. Beyond that, it is reasonable to think that China needs to be included in the process of stopping the proliferation of medium- and long-range missiles and nuclear and chemical weapons. Thus, it is clearly more in the interests of the United States and Japan to be engaged with China rather than disengaged—as a sort of balancing and mediating factor—and to encourage the Chinese leadership's modernization program and maintain ties with the regime than to isolate China from the world.

Any attempt at forecasting the future political and security balance of the Pacific basin requires a thorough analysis of developing economic ties among the Asian Pacific nations. In this regard, our study goes well beyond the usual assessment of intra-Asian trade and the familiar theme of a U.S.-Japanese "trade war," to demonstrate how present bilateral relations transcend old patterns and are expanding to global dimensions. This phenomenon is especially evident in the fact that Japan's assistance in alleviating the international debt problem has become crucial and Japan will soon be the world's largest supplier of overseas development assistance.

In contrast to such positive developments, we report that Soviet economic activities in the region remain comparatively insignificant, that the much advertised perestroika has had little expansive effect on trade between the Soviet Union and its Asian partners. The special economic zones in the Soviet Far East envisioned by Gorbachev are still on the drawing board, and Vladivostok remains essentially a Soviet military base rather than a gateway to world economic opportunity.

China's economic future now seems equally problematic. Deng Xiaping's decade-old "open-door" reform policy came to a temporary halt following the June 1989 crisis. But even before that event, there were many signs that China's transition from central planning to a market-oriented economy was having destabilizing effects that might ultimately hamper economic modernization. Nevertheless, despite its persistent denouncement of "bourgeois liberalism and liberal values," the present Chinese government continues to assure Western business that it welcomes foreign trade and investment. No one has a crystal ball to predict the future, but the prospect of continued foreign access to China—the largest market in Asia—is likely to remain as important to all the other Pacific rim nations, including the United States, as it will to China itself.

Certainly, in addition to those outlined above, there are other crucial issues ripe for scrutiny. Furthermore, the geopolitical stakes are high enough to warrant a careful and sustained examination of alternative futures for the Asian Pacific: the emerging risks and opportunities, the policy options, the security considerations, and the ever changing economic patterns.

For the pursuit of such insights and alternatives in preparing this anthology, we were fortunate to work with an outstanding group of experts from China, Japan, and the United States. From the People's Republic of China, Minister Qian Yongnian, a seasoned diplomat, offers an authoritative summation of political and economic developments in his country. The study group also includes Dr. Hua Di, now an innovative Senior Research Fellow at Stanford University's International Strategic Institute, as well as the strategist, Pan Zhenqiang, Deputy Director of the Institute for Strategic Studies, National Defense University, Beijing. Their contributions to this volume merit close reader attention.

Among the high-level Japanese representation in our research group is Dr. Shinkichi Eto, the dean of Japanese political science, who offers a useful analysis of the Asian situation; and Minister Counselor Ryozo Kato of the Japanese Embassy in Washington, D.C., who helps us to understand the present and future roles and missions of the Japanese Self-Defense Forces.

One of the best informed of American East Asia specialists, Ambassador Stapleton Roy, affords a considered view of the expected power shifts in East Asia between now and the end of this century. Admiral Edward B. Baker, Jr., Commander of U.S. Amphibious Group Three, projects the long-term prospects for U.S. military relationships in East Asia. Dr. James Auer, Director of the United States-Japan Center at Vanderbilt University, concentrates on the global influence of Japanese defense efforts. Edward Ross, Special Assistant for China in the Office of the Secretary of Defense, summarizes and explains the extremely complicated process of evolving U.S.-China military relations. My good friend Dr. Ronald Aqua, of the United States-Japan Foundation, turns his sparkling mind to an analysis of the intricate history of Japan's economic growth.

The preparation and completion of this work would have been beyond my powers without the contributions of this illustrious study group; indeed, all credit for the enlightenment afforded by this book should go to this group, individually and collectively. On my part, I assume responsibility for any errors that may have crept into the text during the editing process. If this work contributes to a deeper appreciation of the forces shaping the future of the Asian Pacific, I shall consider my own efforts as coordinator/editor well rewarded.

I am especially grateful to my style editor, Carole Norton, my special assistant, Jean Johnson, and my graduate assistant, Tan Tsai. I would like to express many thanks to Jill Keeley of the University Press of America, Inc., for her help in seeing the book through publication. And, for generous financial support, I would like to express my appreciation to the Japan-U.S. Friendship Commission. Finally, to my wife, Julianna, who was always at my side with advice and constructive criticism and always willing to share with me the burdens of creating a book, I am most thankful.

Janos Radvanyi
Starkville, Mississippi
January 1990

1

The Changing Asian Pacific—An Introduction
Janos Radvanyi

It may be premature to proclaim the twenty-first century "The Age of the Pacific." There can be no question, however, that the rising economic power of Pacific Asia has clearly begun to influence the strategic posture of the major powers in the region, and thus to alter the worldwide pattern of strategic relations. In pursuit of new answers to an array of domestic economic challenges, all of the present-day major powers most influential in the region—the United States, Japan, China, and the Soviet Union—appear to be moving toward a modification and moderation of previous bilateral and multilateral security relations.

These shifts by the major powers, of course, cannot fail to affect, and be affected by, the domestic priorities and security postures of emerging powers in the region, especially those of the Newly Industrialized Countries (NICs). Democratization in South Korea and the Philippines, economic dynamism in most of the ASEAN nations, planned economic reconstruction in Vietnam, impending leadership transition in North Korea—each of these developments challenges the capacity of all nations of the region to accommodate to altered regional interactions. It is too early yet to say whether any or all of the emerging nations will accomplish their domestic tasks of transition successfully. But, clearly for a great many of them, the process of transition is already well under way, together with a detectable trend toward expanding international cooperation. Equally clear is the special attention the two superpowers are according to evolving strategic and economic realities in the Asian Pacific arena. Europe no longer dominates the thinking of U.S. and Soviet foreign policy makers to the extent that it once did. Instead, they are increasingly focusing on risks and opportunities emerging in the Pacific Basin. In this sense, global patterns of strategic interaction are increasingly reflecting changes in Pacific Asia.

In retrospect, the region has shown a remarkable resilience over the years since World War II. Besides Europe, no other region of the world has demonstrated a greater capacity to generate and accommodate change or to sustain developmental dynamism. Not only has Japan emerged within the last twenty years as a genuine economic superpower, but the "Four Tigers of Asia"—the Republic of Korea, Taiwan, Singapore, and Hong Kong—have consistently achieved annual growth rates over that period which place them among the fastest growing economies of the world. Even such lesser developed economies as Malaysia, Indonesia, and Thailand have posted gains sufficient to invite the envy of Third World nations in all other regions. In China, where market-oriented reforms instituted by the post-Mao leadership have produced annual growth rates in GNP approaching 10 percent since 1982, energies are stirring that may catalyze fundamental changes in the economic and political landscape in the Pacific Basin.

ECONOMIC DEVELOPMENT

Political transformations initiated by economic dynamism in the Asian Pacific region already have had far reaching consequences for individual nations in the region and for the regional system in general. Among the many developing nations, a trend toward political pluralism and the emergence of democratic institutions and liberalization can be observed. Among the communist nations, mounting popular domestic demands have created pressures for economic reforms and some degree of liberalization. So far, the effect of domestic demand has been seen most dramatically in China at least until the June 1989 tragic events at Tiananmen Square, but there are signs of similar changes on the horizon in the Soviet Union. Vietnam, with its economy devastated by forty years of war and communist mismanagement, seems to be turning its efforts toward economic reform and away from hostility to its neighbors.[1] One can only speculate as to what pressures for change might be unleashed when North Korea embarks on the transition to its post-Kim Il Sung era. Unofficial representatives of the North Korean government have expressed interest in normalizing relations with the United States; meanwhile Washington, with Beijing's encourage-ment, has disclosed plans to ease the U.S. trade embargo against North Korea and to facilitate cultural exchange and private visits by academicians.

In recent decades the leaders of virtually all these nations have been forced to the recognition that a peaceful international environment is essential to economic reform and development at home. As a consequence, a discernible tendency toward caution and conciliation has emerged to modify if not to replace the norms of hostility and conflict that so long characterized regional relations. The abatement of Sino-Soviet hostilities and the Soviet Union's recent diplomatic and trade overtures to Japan provide apt examples of this trend. In short, the cultivation of economic opportunity is replacing pursuit of (or defense against) military adventurism as the dominant modality for international relations in the region.

Throughout much of the last decade, the United States benefited in some measure from productive bilateral relations with all the nations of the region except North Korea, the People's Republic of Mongolia, and Vietnam. Intense and wide ranging cooperation among the United States, Japan, and even China gained enhanced significance as expanded economic ties and interests complemented common security concerns arising from the Soviet military presence in Asia. In addition, bilateral U.S.-Japan, U.S.-South Korea, and U.S.-China arrangements encompassing trade, financial, scientific, and technological interchange, expanded considerably, again owing largely to a confluence of economic and security concerns. Conversely, the impressive progress of the NICs of Asia—South Korea, Taiwan, Singapore, and Hong Kong—was driven in no small part by access to the vast and lucrative American consumer market. Indeed, the success of these vigorous contenders in world markets has been a major factor sustaining the economic dynamism of the entire region.

In Japan, the smooth transition between administrations bodes well for a continuation of four decades of established cooperation between Japan and the United States. The change in command has created opportunities for new approaches to old problems. For example, progress at negotiations to ease Japanese restrictions on certain American imports and to improve better American access to Japanese public work projects so far has helped prevent trade tensions from erupting into full-scale economic strife.

In the late 1980s U.S.-Japan economic cooperation produced a two-way trade of $112 billion. During that period 20 percent of all U.S. agricultural exports went to Japan, and an excess of $25 billion in direct Japanese investments in the United States eventuated in approximately 200,000 new jobs for Americans. Today, one-third of America's budget deficit is financed by financial institutions headquartered in Japan. Under the Bush administration, U.S.-Japanese interactions continue apace. Yet economic tensions between the United States and Japan will go on with some of the debates gaining heat. For example, many will not stop to question the fairness of Japan's trading policies and practices vis-à-vis so close an ally as the United States. Already the fact that America's trade deficit with Japan failed to decline substantially following a sharp appreciation of the yen against the dollar has contributed to U.S. dissatisfaction. Such strains can only intensify should budget deficits and other economic hazards trigger deep recession or some other crisis in America. Moreover, the overt and hidden conflicts present in trade relations will inevitably spill over into the bilateral security arena, where issues of burden sharing are already causing much debate. Here a last minute American change in heart concerning military hardware related to technology transfer—as evidenced by the agreement to build the FSX jet (the Japanese version of the American F-16 fighter plane) complicated cooperation.

In recent years the United States has become China's second largest trading partner, trailing only Japan.[2] The United States provided investment capital, technology, and managerial expertise for China's economic modernization, much of it in aid of building up the PRC's industrial infrastructure. China, for its part, has shown it has much to offer the United States in areas such as medicine, scientific experimentation, and earthquake prediction. In addition, China has become a major supplier of textile products and other soft goods for American consumers. Regardless of the present strained political relations, over the long run the United States stands to benefit greatly by this expanding two-way flow: the greater the U.S. role in China's modernization, the greater will be its leverage with a nation that is certain to exert a major influence on the pace and direction of future developments in the Asian Pacific arena. China, too, stands to benefit. For China, closer cooperation with the United States is tied to the vital economic objectives of industrial modernization and market expansion.

As for China-Japan economic cooperation, efforts toward improved trade relations have been overshadowed recently by Chinese complaints that Japan is more interested in China as a market for its consumer goods than as a beneficiary of its advanced industrial technology. This negative perception was somewhat offset recently when Tokyo announced that China will become the number one recipient of the Japanese foreign aid program (Overseas Development Aid, ODA). Even so, and despite the fact that Japan had not altered its policy after the June events and continued to be in fact China's number one trading partner, much remains to be done to dissipate Chinese suspicions of Japan and to convince Beijing that Japan is genuinely interested in China's success.

The Chinese have also sought to enhance bilateral economic relations with the Soviet Union. Sino-Soviet trade in 1987 approached a $3 billion valuation, most of it in the form of bartered manufactures and commodities. This trade must be considered minuscule when compared to Western contributions to China's modernization and to the PRC's own export achievements, to which the manufacturing contribution alone has expanded 13 percent annually over the last six years (1982-1988). The diplomatic implications of renewed Sino-Soviet trade cannot be ignored, however, and the leadership in both nations appears intent upon strengthening mutual economic and cultural ties over the next decade. While reasons behind the normalization of Sino-Soviet relations are clear (easing of tensions), China's position in the international communist movement is ambiguous. The restoration of the CCP relations with numerous non-ruling communist parties and the resumption of party-to-party ties with Soviet bloc countries—Poland and the German Democratic Republic in 1986, and Hungary, Czechoslovakia, and Bulgaria a year later—might be interpreted as a convergence with Soviet interest and a calculated counter-balance to China's overtures to the West. But these restorations could also be intended as an ideological counterweight to Moscow's influence in the international communist movement. However, in the midst of the dramatic and unanticipated 1989 East-European revolutions and the formation of Presidential power of Gorbachev, party-to-party relation became a paradox and irrelevant residue of the past.

Moscow has yet to allocate to Asia either resources or policy attention in amounts sufficient to make the Soviet Union a major actor in the Asian Pacific economy. So far, new Russian economic projects have been concentrated in Western Siberia, not in the Soviet Far East, and these projects have aimed mainly at exploration and exploitation of natural resources. So long as *perestroika* brings more hardships than boons and domestic food production remains a major unresolved problem, Soviet aspirations for a greater role in the economy of the Pacific Basin may be unrealistic. Soviet industry, largely outmoded and beset by structural and technological shortcomings, seems an unlikely competitor for the thoroughly modern industries of Japan or the dynamic capabilities of the Four Tigers. In a region where economic success rests on enterprise and competition, the Soviet Union has little to offer. Even if the Gorbachev regime can establish its much heralded Far Eastern Free Economic Zones, few Asian investors are likely to be lured by the incentive. Nevertheless, the Soviets have been actively courting foreign investment in the hope that their new joint venture laws will attract Asian interest in locating production facilities on Soviet soil.

Finally, if any one development can be said to symbolize the dramatic turn of events in the Asian Pacific, it is the emergence of Asia's Newly Industrialized Countries as world market competitors. In the years 1986-1988 the economies of Singapore, Hong Kong, South Korea, and Taiwan all grew by more than 8 percent annually. (In the same period in America and the countries of the European Economic Community, the growth rate never exceeded 3 percent.) The growth of the NICs' financial power is no less exceptional. The 1988 $73 billion foreign exchange reserves of Taiwan (third largest in the world) and South Korea assure these countries economic strength far beyond their physical sizes. The increased exports of manufactured goods from the NICs and the developing nations of the Asian Pacific have made firm in-roads not only into the lucrative American and European markets but also into Japan. Indeed, since 1985 the biggest increases in manufactured exports to Japan have been posted not by America, but by Taiwan, Thailand, and South Korea. Moreover, Thailand, Malaysia, and other developing countries in Asia today offer attractively low-cost labor for foreign, mainly Japanese, investors.

SECURITY RELATIONS

In the security area, the major concern of the United States and its Japanese and South Korean allies in the 1970s and 1980s was the Soviet military buildup in the Pacific. Understandably so, for one-third of all the Soviet Union's military might was deployed east of the Urals and poised against the Pacific Coast of North America and the major Asian countries. The Soviet Pacific fleet, with headquarters at Vladivostok, was and still is the largest of the Soviet navy's four fleets, commanding 2 carriers, 12 cruisers, 12 destroyers, 47 frigates, and 112 submarines. The Soviet Far Eastern Strategic Forces in 1988 included 366 submarine-launched ballistic missiles, 440 intercontinental missiles (SS-11, SS-17, and SS-18), 132 intermediate range ballistic missiles, and 160 bombers.[3]

China was also apprehensive about the Soviet military presence in Asia, despite Mikhail Gorbachev's commitment to *Glasnost* and "new thinking," for the same intermediate range ballistic missiles that threatened Tokyo and Okinawa can also threaten Beijing. What is more, at the end of 1987 approximately 55 Soviet army divisions still were deployed along the Sino-Soviet and Sino-Mongolian borders.

To counter this ominous Soviet presence, Japan in 1988 had only its Self-Defense Forces (a total of 245,000 regulars), and the role of the Japanese navy and air force was restricted to defense of territory, air space, and vital sea lines of communications within a range extending 1,000 miles outward from Japan. China's armed forces numbered 3,200,000 regulars in 1988[4], but its navy and air force were technologically inadequate and its strategic capabilities severely limited. Under these circumstances only the nuclear umbrella and conventional forces of the United States[5] provided a unified military presence capable of deterring Soviet threat in the region. This U.S. presence of course is augmented by American security arrangements with Japan and South Korea as protection against possible Soviet actions.

On the Soviet side, however, present Soviet policy, in contrast with that of the past few decades, seems to be aimed at a more conciliatory, balanced, and sophisticated approach to regional problems of the Far East. An analysis of recent Soviet policy statements and actions strongly indicates that neutralization of the Russian eastern flank and tranquility along the long Russo-Mongolian-Chinese border have been accorded high priority in Soviet diplomatic strategies.

Since Gorbachev's 1986 Vladivostok speech, the Soviets have softened their stance toward East Asia in general and stepped up friendly overtures to China, Japan, and even South Korea. They have also taken steps toward a qualified accommodation of China's "Three Obstacles" in the course of a renewed political dialogue with Beijing. Undoubtedly, behind these Soviet overtures lies an agonizing dilemma. If the Soviet Union supports China, it risks antagonizing India and Vietnam, but if it stands by idly, it risks losing China completely to the influence of the United States and its allies. The choice reflects Soviet priorities. The seven-point proposal offered by Gorbachev in September 1988 at Krasnoyarsk gives further credence to the notion that the USSR is an active participant in the political and economic affairs of the Asian Pacific. Gorbachev's suggestion that the Soviet Union "is consistently looking for points of contact" with the United States on problems of the Asian and Pacific regions[6] reinforces this perception.

The central theme of Gorbachev's Far Eastern plan, however, clearly revolves around normalized relations with China, as evidenced by the May 1989 Soviet-Chinese summit coupled with his warnings about the expansion of Japan's military strength. In serenading the Asian Pacific by offering plans for reduced military tension, by promising special trading zones along the Soviet seaboard and proposing the establishment of a China-Japan-Soviet tripartite economic cooperation in agricultural production, he is courting China primarily. No Soviet concession so far has been offered to Japan in the dispute over the northern islands in the Sea of Okhtosk, probably out of fear that this would set a precedent for other territorial revisions and because the Soviet's military installations on two of the four disputed islands are considered vital to a secure exit from the Sea of Okhtosk for the Pacific fleet. Foreign Minister Edward Shevardnadze's visit to Tokyo in December 1988 produced no progress in this territorial dispute.

THE PROSPECTS

Recognizing the dynamism and potential of the Asian Pacific, both superpowers are certain to follow closely the complex and diversified trends that shape the region, both ever aware that their rivalry, in that region, is far from over.

Operating in the Pacific Basin over the coming decade, the United States will enjoy many clear advantages over the Soviet Union. America will continue to be a major market for Asian exports and a major provider of opportunities for safe large-scale investment for Japan, the NICs, and other countries in the region. Expanding U.S. service industries are likely to find a receptive market here, and international movements of capital and technology will enhance the importance of the U.S. role among allies and friends in the region. Finally, of course, a flexible and diversified U.S. military presence will continue as a check on the Soviet military threat.

For the Soviet Union, the possibilities are more restricted. There will be some room for economic cooperation between the Soviet Union and the Asian Pacific countries, with joint ventures the most likely avenue of interaction; however, the nations of Asia are doubtful about Soviet reliability in business ventures and the long-range safety of investments in Eastern Siberia and other Soviet territories. The real question mark, though, lies in the evolution of Soviet detente policy. There is a widely held belief in Asia that the Soviet Union is a superpower only in the military dimension, that unless its failing economy can be revitalized, it will become a second-rate power in the 1990s and beyond. It is also a fact that after three and one-half years of *perestroika* the Russian home front is still in shambles and the standard of living has actually declined.

Many Asian countries, among them most importantly China and Japan, are simply not convinced that the Soviet leadership will be able to place economic reform ahead of military modernization. They see no convincing evidence that the funds released by lowered military spending will be used to build benign industries instead of new weaponry systems, new generations of missiles, and super submarines. Long exposure to Soviet threats and intimidation has nourished the suspicion in Pacific Asia that the much heralded "new detente" will prove to be only a breathing period to enable Soviet economic retrenchment to renewed expansionism. And finally, there is considerable doubt that Gorbachev will be able to bring to fruition his economic reforms in the Soviet Union. Or, might he not be forced out of power first, or might he return to some form of centralized control in order to stay in power?

Apart from the ongoing competition between the superpowers, the other central features in the changing dynamics of the Asian-Pacific area will be the strengthening influence of Japan and the evolution of the People's Republic of China. Policy trends in these two countries can have significant impact on the region's strategic balance. Should China attain to the economic strength envisioned by its present leadership it will be assured a major political role in Asia. In addition, there is perhaps a 50-50 chance that the modernization now under way in China could eventuate in an all new strategic balance in the region. Meanwhile, Chinese economic cooperation with the United States is likely to slow down for a while as Beijing reverts to Marxist roots. Yet China still needs American high technology and managerial expertise for its modernization process. Chinese purchases of U.S. defensive armaments, avionic components, and anti-submarine torpedoes is presently suspended, but for how long, nobody can predict. At the same time, the American as well as the Chinese governments have taken care to isolate certain intelligence sharings from the ups and down of political relations. The electronic listening posts in Xinjiang Autonomous Region and elsewhere are still monitoring nuclear tests and seismic disturbances in Soviet territories. Also, China will remain vigilant regarding any expansion of Japan's Self-Defense Forces. Even the moderate boost accorded Japan's 1988 military budget is certain to be seen by some hard-liners in the Chinese military establishment as a signal of reviving Japanese "militarism."

In Japan, a significant gap between economic and military capabilities will persist. Constitutional impediments, domestic political pressures, and the concerns of neighboring countries (especially China) will continue to impose constraints on Japan's military build-up. Even if Japan continues to allocate a very small portion of its GNP to defense, however, its high-tech capabilities will inevitably make it a significant military power. Asia will also witness profound changes in Japan's participation in international affairs in general and in its regional foreign aid activities in particular.

The strengthening of Japan and the resurgence of China will have important implications for the United States in that both will foster a certain erosion of America's dominant economic position. Although protectionism could further undermine U.S. influence, it seems likely that brisk international movements of capital, technology, and goods can benefit America as well as its Asian allies. Japan's economic planning agency has forecast that between now and the year 2000 the U.S. economy will grow more slowly than that of Japan, so that the purchasing power parity basis will shift in favor of Japan. If and when that occurs, Japan will need even more of the American market, and the interdependence of the two economies will increase accordingly.

On the political front, the era of American stewardship over Japan and South Korea will end. A new and more natural partnership, redefined military ties, and a new course of political interaction among the United States and its Asian allies will take shape. Japan's greater role in world affairs will generate momentums to hasten this change. South Korea's interest in establishing relations with the Soviet Union is likely to prove disappointing for Seoul in the long run. Meanwhile, however, until South Korea can handle its own defense against North Korea and until North Korea gives up its military pressure tactics to destabilize the South, the American defense shield should continue, perhaps with an alternating combined forces command structure (within which supreme command will not necessarily be vested in a senior American general). In the Philippines, the possible loss of American military bases at Subic Bay and elsewhere could create serious security problems for Washington. Other problems can be expected for America in Indonesia, for example, or in Malaysia and Thailand. But ultimately, political necessity and strategic considerations may compel the United States and its Asian allies and friends to submerge their differences to assure a continuation of the basic defense policy they have followed since the Vietnam War.

The NICs of Asia seem destined for major importance in the world economy. By their introduction of structural adjustments, their search for growth through exports and investments, and their responsiveness to domestic demands they can contribute greatly to the health and prosperity of Asia. The developing countries of Asia likewise are expected to move toward economic strength, and even the Philippines, despite the serious economic and political hurdles it faces, embodies impressive capabilities for growth. Although a formal trade zone in the Asian Pacific has yet to be established, the groundwork is laid and with the intra-Asian trade growing at double-digit rates at the close of the 1980s it seems probable a Pacific economic community will become a reality by the close of the first decade of the twenty-first century.

Earlier than that, by the turn of the century, a new generation of leadership will have come to power in Asia, a generation of different educational background, political philosophy, and approach to economic problems than its predecessors. The men who forged the present-day politico-economic structures of the region—men like China's Deng Xiaoping, Indonesia's Suharto, and Singapore's Lee Kuan Yew—will have stepped aside. Their passing will affect the future of their nations in both positive and negative directions.

The Korean Peninsula presents a striking example of contemporary forces in Asia. South Korea has carried out a formidable economic expansion and is going through a political liberalization, while in North Korea, the People's Republic remains economically stagnant, and politically encapsulated in communist dictatorship. Not only in China, but also in the Soviet Union and the Eastern Bloc countries leaders are beginning to see the advantages of cooperation with South Korea. Even so, the Korean Peninsula remains a powder keg in the Asian Pacific. It is perhaps the only spot in the region where polarization is still so rigid, with relations between North and South marked by unremitting hostility, mistrust, and misunderstanding. These tensions may yield somewhat in the coming decade to pressures from the superpowers and from other major regional powers. But equally important will be the tension of the future North-South dialogue, which in turn will depend largely on the results of North Korea's transition into the post-Kim Il Sung era, on the makeup of the new leadership and its willingness and ability to pursue serious efforts to resolve the deadlock.

The pervasive transformations now in progress throughout Pacific Asia may prove conducive to regional peace, stability, and prosperity, or they may foreshadow renewed conflicts, tensions, and instabilities. Certainly the stakes are high enough for all the powers involved to warrant a careful examination of the forces at play in the region, the risks and opportunities each presents, and the policy options available for the pursuit of preferred alternatives. The present collection of essays from eminent observers adds up to a rare and illuminating discourse, for it explores the implications of changing power relations in Pacific Asia from many points of view and thus gives unusual breadth as well as depth to our understanding. What emerges is an integrated forecast of how economic developments in the region are likely to structure future strategic frameworks, how new opportunities might create new risks and vice versa. What also emerges is a kaleidoscopic appraisal of the ways in which the powers of the region, individually and in concert, might adapt or fail to adapt their policies because of any number of domestic constraints. In sum, it is hoped that this timely exploration of possibilities for Pacific Asia will contribute to enlightened policy making in the decades ahead.

NOTES

[1.]Reportedly, Vietnam is beginning to withdraw its troops from Cambodia and pledged to remove all its troops by September 1989. *Wall Street Journal* (January 13, 1989), p. 1.

[2.]According to U.S. figures, the two-way trade between the United States and China totaled $10.4 billion in 1987, Chinese figures set the total at $7.8 billion. The discrepancy arises from goods that pass through third countries. By the end of 1988, U.S. businesses had set up 500 joint ventures backed by a total committed investment of about $3.25 billion, and China had set up more than 140 trade-related enterprises in the United States. "U.S.-Chinese Exchanges," AP, Beijing (December 31, 1988).

[3.]The Military Balance, 1988-1989 (London: International Institute for Strategic Studies, 1988), p. 43.

[4.]Ibid., pp. 147, 164.

[5.]U.S. forces under the Pacific Command include Army, Air Force, and Navy personnel stationed in Hawaii, the Philippines, Japan, South Korea, Guam, Australia, and Diego Garcia.

6. Mikhail Gorbachev, Speech at Krasnoyarsk, as reported by Beijing XINHUA Domestic Service (16 September 1988), reprinted in *FBIS-CHI-88-181* (19 September 1988), p. 10.

2

Political and Economic Prospects for East Asia in the 1990s and Beyond
J. Stapleton Roy

The outlook for power shifts in East Asia between now and the end of this century has generated a great deal of attention, and a broad range of conclusions. Some observers foresee an evolution toward a complex multipower system by the year 2000, with a significantly weakened American influence. Many see Japan emerging as the major economic and political force in East Asia and forecast that the yen will replace the dollar as the region's dominant currency. Already, it is pointed out, the United States is placing increasing reliance on Japan to provide foreign aid to strategically placed countries around the world, even to the Philippines, for which the United States has traditionally assumed a proprietary responsibility. The pessimists among the prognosticators also believe that United States-Japanese trade tensions, aggravated by short-sighted U.S. fiscal policies, are likely to become permanent and that Japan, in adjusting, will develop an overall national strategy attuned to greater independence of action. A key question mark over such projections is whether Japan will seek a strong military capability, possibly one bolstered with nuclear weapons.

Others postulate that the People's Republic of China(PRC) will emerge as the Asian superpower of the future. For example, the January 1988 Report of the Commission on Integrated Long-Term Strategy,[1] foresees the possibility that over the next twenty years the growth in the Chinese economy will outpace that in the United States, Europe, or the Soviet Union, so that China may emerge as the world's second or third largest economy, and capable of becoming a military superpower. Whether or not such projections seem exaggerated, they highlight a point that deserves attention: over the last ten years (1978-1988), China has exceeded all earlier predictions in achieving a rapid and sustained rate of economic development.

The Commission Report goes on to detail a number of other developments that could have great relevance for East Asia. One is the diminishing
U.S. ability, worldwide, to gain agreement for timely access, including bases
and overflight rights, to areas threatened by Soviet aggression. Another is
the increasing difficulty, and political cost encountered by the United States
in its efforts to maintain bases in the Third World. Meanwhile, the Report
notes, Soviet military power in East Asia is growing, and thereby increasing
the threat to Japan and South Korea in the north, while farther south, the
continued Soviet military presence in Vietnam adds tension to debates about
the future of the U.S. bases in the Philippines. All these considerations raise
the possibility of a major strategic shift in Southeast Asia.

According to many of these projections, the outlook for the United
States is uncertain at best. According to Professor Paul Kennedy and others,
the United States is a declining great power that is overextended in its
commitments and lacking in economic strength to meet all the challenges of
the commitments undertaken during its period of world supremacy. Kennedy
argues that, "given the worldwide array of military liabilities which the
United States has assumed since 1945, its capacity to carry those burdens is
obviously less than it was several decades ago, when its share of global
manufacturing and GNP was much larger, its agriculture was not in crisis,
its balance of payments was far healthier, the government budget was also
in balance, and it was not so heavily in debt to the rest of the world."

Proceeding from this analysis, "the task facing American statesmen over
the next decades is to . . . 'manage' affairs so that the relative erosion of the
United States' position takes place slowly and smoothly, and is not accelerated by policies which bring merely short-term advantage but longer-term
disadvantage." It follows, then, that the task of diplomacy is "to find new
allies, settle differences with potential foes, withdraw from overextended
positions, and encourage friendly nations to share more of the burden—all
this in order to bring the country's commitments more into harmony with its
capacities." Such projections are not merely of concern to Americans but
may be even more alarming to countries like Japan that have relied both on
the strength of the U.S. economy and on the U.S. security shield. One
Japanese report in 1989, for example, predicted that America's weakened
manufacturing base, loss of technological superiority, and protectionist
sentiment could do major harm to Japan.

It should come as no surprise that those who subscribe to such
projections, and to the presumed policy prescriptions that flow from them,

tend toward a gloomy view of the future. Obviously, if the United States were to accept the propositions that what the future holds in store are a loosening of the U.S.-Japan alliance, a search for new alignments in Asia, and a lessening of the stabilizing U.S. security presence in the region, there would indeed be grounds for alarm. In particular, the prospect of even a partial American security withdrawal from Asia is troublesome because, as most observers agree, no other country is now capable of fully assuming America's present role. In part, this lack is a result of the post World War II reluctance of Germany and Japan to assume important political responsibilities outside their respective regions coupled with their legal restraints against military buildup. In any case, it is equally true that most countries in Asia would be disturbed by indications that Japan was preparing to step into the U.S. security role in the region.

As these examples illustrate, the task of peering into the future not only presents many challenges but also can lead to some disturbing conclusions. Fortunately, human beings are notably fallible as predictors of things to come. By way of illustrating this point, one need only review a few developments in East Asia during the last decade in the wake of the U.S. withdrawal from Vietnam. Contrary to assumptions in some quarters, Hanoi's leaders were *not* satisfied with national reunification and sought instead to impose their hegemony over all Indochina. Nevertheless, and again contrary to assumptions in other quarters, the ASEAN dominoes did not fall but rather developed a remarkable cohesion that transformed the organization into a model regional grouping. China turned into an implacable foe of its former ally, Hanoi, and assumed a leading role in blocking further Vietnamese expansionism. The United States remained engaged in Asia and did not revert to the isolationism that some had feared. And the newly industrialized economies of East Asia continued to provide the world with a dramatic demonstration of what good leadership and sensible economic policies can accomplish.

From all this it should be clear that projections into the future can be no more accurate than the validity of the assumptions on which they are based. But it is equally true that any look into the future must begin with a realistic evaluation of the present. From this standpoint the United States, despite its budgetary difficulties, is well positioned to deal with the challenges of the next decade in Asia. U.S. policy in East Asia and the Pacific has been remarkably successful over the past decade, not so much because the United States has initiated favorable developments in the area as because its policies have been compatible with and reinforced the dominant regional trends toward rapid economic development and more democratic political systems.

With a few exceptions, such as the final years of Marcos rule in the Philippines, U.S. friends and allies have been stable and prosperous and have made good use of America's wide-open market to fuel their own export-oriented development strategies, with the result that East Asia in recent years has surpassed all other areas of the world in GNP growth and increased international trade. Its leaders have been generally capable and forward looking.

Ideologically, moreover, the United States has been on the offensive. In the 1980s, unlike the 1950s when Maoist China exerted an ideological attraction for many in Asia as a model for developing countries, the Cultural Revolution has thoroughly discredited the socialist model and the negative examples of Vietnam and North Korea have driven home the lesson. Today, governments and intellectuals alike are attracted by the economic successes of countries that have based their development strategies on market forces rather than central planning.

Of paramount importance to the U.S. regional position was the establishment in 1979 of U.S.-PRC diplomatic relations, which permitted a rapid expansion of U.S. contacts with China and provided a framework for managing and containing remaining differences over Taiwan. The far-reaching positive transformation of U.S.-China relations over the last decade has paralleled China's own move toward stability and moderation. Indeed, these two processes have been mutually reinforcing and have led to the friendly, mature relationship between China and the United States which was confirmed by Foreign Minister Wu's visit to the United States in March 1988. The U.S. relationship with China became strained following the tragic events at Beijing's Tiananmen Square. But common strategic concerns and potential mutual benefits across a broad spectrum of economic, commercial, cultural, and political areas might reverse the negative trend in time.

Because of the congruence between the U.S. policies and the success of most East Asian countries in dealing with their domestic problems, improving the well-being of their peoples, and containing sources of tension, the United States has been in a relatively strong position in East Asia throughout most of the 1980s. However, these are not grounds for complacency. Changes are under way for a variety of reasons, some beyond control of the United States and some related to its own policies.

Economic problems are assuming increasing importance in U.S. relations with friends and allies in the region. For various reasons, U.S. trade deficits with East Asia have reached unsustainable levels in recent years; indeed, the outcome of current efforts by the United States to find effective measures to address its massive trade imbalances with Asian economies may well determine its ability to preserve an open world trading system. Correction of these imbalances will force alterations in those development strategies which are geared to running massive trade surpluses with the United States. Over time, these alterations will reduce—at least in relative terms—the importance of the U.S. market to the affected countries. Some of them may have difficulty making the adjustment, especially in light of the fact that U.S. aid inputs to the region have now shrunk to a post-war low.

Obviously, the United States is not about to withdraw altogether from East Asia or to abandon its major interests in the peace, stability, and prosperity of the region. Even if the United States corrects its trade imbalance with the region, it will remain a giant market for East Asian countries, and it will continue to be an important source of investment capital. The United States also plays a security role that no other country is equipped to play. However, unless it can maintain current levels of security assistance, the credibility of the U.S. security commitments will be eroded and regional countries will increasingly seek to fill their needs elsewhere, as Thailand has already done by turning to China. American security support for the Philippines and Thailand is particularly critical in this respect.

These changes are occurring at a time when Soviet diplomacy in East Asia has become more active and subtle in the wake of Gorbachev's Vladivostok speech in July 1986 and his Beijing visit in May 1989. Although skeptical of Soviet motives, regional countries have displayed interest in exploring the implications of a fresh Soviet approach to Asian problems. Put another way, Gorbachev has managed to kindle hopes among regional leaders that the Soviet Union may become relevant to the search for a solution in Cambodia and for a strategy that can lower tensions on the Korean Peninsula. As regional countries scramble to diversify their trading patterns, they are likely also to explore the Soviet Union's potential as a trading partner.

This trend is already evident in Sino-Soviet relations, which have now improved to a point where policy makers can no longer assume that Beijing and Moscow will automatically adopt divergent positions on regional issues.

Chinese leaders have made no secret of their hope that Gorbachev's concentration on correcting Soviet domestic economic deficiencies will strengthen Soviet incentives to seek a period of relaxed international tensions.

This analysis suggests that although significant changes may be in store in East Asia between now and the end of the century, America need not jump to pessimistic conclusions about the ability of regional countries, as well as the United States, to manage the process in a skillful and enlightened fashion. In fact, one of the signal characteristics of East Asia in recent years has been the ability of its leaders to take advantage of opportunities and to create favorable options where none seemed to exist before. This adaptability has surfaced in the ASEAN response to Vietnamese aggression in Cambodia, the normalization of U.S.-PRC relations, the emergence of the Aquino government in the Philippines, the peaceful political transition in South Korea, and the gradual lowering of barriers between Taiwan and the Mainland.

Based on this record, a healthy degree of optimism seems warranted. For one thing, while current U.S. budgetary difficulties are real enough, the capacity of the United States to correct the problem should not be underestimated. In fact, one of the reasons so many earlier predictions floundered is that the forecasters failed to take into account the ability of countries, under wise leaders, to recognize, adjust to, and reverse adverse trends.

Many of the more pessimistic assumptions about U.S. economic decline were made before the recent adjustments in the value of the dollar that have increased the competitiveness of U.S. exports. Prospects for fending off the worst forms of protectionist legislation have improved, both because of the Reagan administration's firm opposition and because presidential hopeful Gephardt failed to strike a spark with his protectionist campaign appeals. Belatedly, U.S. industrial leaders are also recognizing the need to make U.S. business more competitive. To cite one example, U.S. Steel in early 1988 managed, as a result of painful adjustments, to reduce its labor costs in a five year period from over 50 percent of the sales dollar to less than 20 percent, with a corresponding sharp rise in productivity.

A second point is worth emphasizing. Unlike some other regions of the world, the major powers in the Far East are relatively comfortable with the current security balance and generally welcome the stabilizing role the United States has played. More important, they all recognize that no other country is in a position to assume the same role, and they prefer the U.S. presence to any of the potential alternatives. Accordingly, though the United States may, until it gets its economic house in order, face a period of budgetary stringency in meeting its obligations, there will be severe constraints on any significant alteration in the U.S. role, if only because both the United States and the majority of the regional countries wish the United States to remain constructively engaged.

The Soviet Union may be an exception to the above generalizations. But the Soviet Union has been out of step with most of the positive trends in the region, and now its leaders seem to recognize that if they want to gain greater Soviet acceptance in East Asia, they must end the over-reliance on military force that has burdened Soviet foreign policy. Whether they can muster the courage, the skill, and the domestic cohesion to make these adjustments remains to be seen. For the moment, the most obvious changes have occurred in Moscow's policies towards Europe and its approach to arms control and disarmament issues. But the extraordinary Soviet military buildup in Asia of the last two decades continued unabated, with the focus more recently shifting to enhanced Soviet naval and air capabilities in the Soviet maritime provinces and at Cam Ranh Bay. This shift indeed was the primary reason for the growth of U.S. military strength in the region.

At the same time, one should not dismiss possibilities for a substantial easing of tensions in East Asia over the next decade. The Soviet Union has ended its ill-fated military intervention in Afghanistan with the withdrawal of its last troops in February 1989. There has been hopeful progress in U.S.-Soviet arms reduction talks, and Sino-Soviet border confrontations are less frequent than at any time in the last quarter century. Under these circumstances, should progress be achieved toward a Cambodia settlement, the United States could look forward to an unprecedented period of reduced tension among China, the United States, and the Soviet Union going well beyond most current projections.

This thought has potentially far reaching implications for the whole region. An Afghan resolution would inevitably increase the already existing pressures for a Cambodia settlement. Even though Vietnam stands in no danger of being driven from Cambodia by the resistance forces, its new leaders seem to recognize the opportunity costs they are paying by remaining isolated in one of the economically most dynamic regions in the world and have promised to withdraw all their troops by September 1989. The removal of the Afghan obstacle also will increase incentives for both Moscow and

Beijing to find ways to improve Sino-Soviet relations with respect to Cambodia.

A Cambodian settlement would leave the question of Soviet military deployments along the Sino-Soviet border as the sole remaining obstacle in the way of a restoration of closer ties between Moscow and Beijing. The present strength of the Soviet border forces is excessive by any reasonable standard; thus they can be substantially reduced whenever this would suit Moscow's political purposes. The prospect of an imminent political breakthrough in Sino-Soviet relations would generate strong pressures for a settlement of Sino-Soviet territorial differences by means of relatively minor adjustments along the border. Although such an accommodation would have been unthinkable until recently, both sides have now accepted the principle of "mutual understanding and mutual accommodation" as the basis for a border settlement—a principle that holds open the possibility of trade-offs among disputed sectors.

What would be the implications of such a development for the region? The answer could be generally positive. The same policy of flexibility on territorial issues that could restore "normal" Sino-Soviet political relations could also make it easier for Moscow to contemplate the relatively minor territorial adjustments—i.e., the return of the four islands which make up the northern territories—necessary to improve Soviet relations with Japan. Or to put it another way, it will be harder for Moscow to remain rigid on retaining the territories seized from Japan at the close of World War II once it displays flexibility in a border settlement with China. The constraints on such a development remain significant, to be sure. Nevertheless, the prospect should not be lightly discarded, especially since Gorbachev has displayed a willingness to cast off traditional Soviet behavioral patterns in seeking to shake Soviet diplomacy out of the rigidities of the past.

If and when the Soviet Union is prepared to address the territorial issue with Japan, prospects could once again open up for renewed Japanese interest in the development of Siberian resources. The international environment within which such a development might take place in the 1990s would be quite different from the earlier periods when Japan and the Soviet Union explored possibilities for economic cooperation in Siberia. In the late 1960s and early 1970s, Sino-Soviet tensions were high, and Sino-U.S. relations were far less stable than at present.

Over the next ten years, the Free World might well see leadership changes in North Korea that will at long last put an end to Pyongyang's bizarre and barbaric conduct and draw it into the civilized community of nations. This development, in turn, could bring about substantially reduced tensions on the Korean Peninsula, paving the way for adjustments in the U.S. military engagement in South Korea that would not destabilize the region. These adjustments would have nothing in common with the Carter administration proposals for troop withdrawals from Korea, which alarmed friends of the United States in the region precisely because they were designed to proceed without a prior fundamental improvement in the security environment on the peninsula.

What policy implications for the United States would flow from such far-reaching changes in the East Asian environment over the next ten to twelve years? The answer is that the United States could adjust to developments along these lines without radical or disruptive changes in its approach to the region. The United States would still remain actively involved in East Asia economically, politically, and militarily. However, the costs of its forward deployments could be reduced both in response to favorable developments in the security environment and in recognition of the growing ability of Japan and South Korea to share the burden of deterring aggression.

Obviously, other, less benign scenarios are also possible for the 1990s. Moreover, a substantial relaxation of tensions among the major powers in East Asia would not be without its challenges, especially as younger leaders replace the generation whose attitudes were shaped by World War II. On the home front, one of the factors contributing to the coherence and continuity of U.S. policy in Asia has been a strong domestic consensus in support of the principal components of that policy: the primacy of the U.S.-Japan alliance, the importance of the new relationship of Washington with Beijing, the close U.S. relationship with ASEAN, and the need to retain a strong forward defense position as a contribution to regional stability. The consistency and clarity of U.S. policy could be adversely affected if this consensus were eroded by, say, chronic economic frictions with Japan, a weakening of ASEAN cohesion in the wake of a Cambodia settlement, or ominously altered relations among the major powers in East Asia. Fortunately, such problems are not inevitable, nor are they immune to solution through sound policies. Accordingly, the domestic consensus appears likely to remain intact over the next decade.

There are other imponderables that could alter the course of events in

East Asia. These include the future state of the world economy, as well as China's ability to return to the path of reform and opening to the outside world while maintaining domestic stability and rapid economic growth, the success of the Philippine government in dealing with its domestic problems, the outcome of the U.S.-Philippine base negotiations in 1991, future trends in relations between Chinese on both sides of the Taiwan Strait, the management of the 1997 transition in Hong Kong, Vietnam's willingness to assume a constructive role in the region, future trends in Indonesia, the direction of Soviet policies, and the degree to which Japan becomes more assertive in its behavior.

Based on present realities, those who make pessimistic assumptions about the ability of regional countries to deal successfully with such imponderables are more likely to be off the mark than those of more optimistic mind. It is worth remembering what Winston Churchill said in a time far more perilous than today: "I'm an optimist because there's not much point in anything else." Nor, in conclusion, is there reason to be discouraged by the failures of past efforts to predict the future. Those who have read Barbara Tuchman's fascinating book *The March of Folly* will recall it contains a rich store of examples of opportunities lost, advantages squandered, and tragedies precipitated, because of muddleheaded leadership. After all, in world affairs, leadership, not prognostication, is the determining factor in the fate of nations.

The reason for the central importance of leadership is precisely that one cannot predict the future with absolute assurance. It takes leaders to cope effectively with the constantly changing circumstances that are an integral part of daily life. Fortunate, indeed, are the nations whose leaders are astute enough to recognize dangers and opportunities in advance and to take the necessary steps to deal with them. But the real test of leadership comes in coping with the unanticipated situation which is, if anything, the rule rather than the exception. If the past is prologue to the future, one can take confidence in the fact that in recent years many East Asian leaders have established an excellent record in meeting such challenges.

NOTES

[1.]*Discriminate Deterrence*, Report of the Commission on Integrated Long Term Strategy (U.S. Government Printing Office, Washington, D.C., 1988).

3

Politics and Economic Prosperity in East Asia
Shinkichi Eto

In 1980 the dollar volume of U.S. trade with countries in Asia and the Pacific became roughly equal to that of U.S. trade with the countries of Western Europe. By 1986 the balance had tipped toward the Pacific to the extent of some $30 billion. If this trend continues, by 1995 U.S. trade with the Asian-Pacific region may be twice as great as that with Western Europe.

Meanwhile, within the Asian-Pacific region, four of the six countries in the world categorized by the United Nations as "newly industrialized countries (NICs)"—Singapore, Hong Kong, South Korea and Taiwan—are today registering high economic growth, as are Thailand, Indonesia and Malaysia. In contrast, the two NICs outside the region, Brazil and Mexico, are beset with financial difficulties.

In addition to the capitalist countries of the Asian-Pacific region, the socialist People's Republic of China, which for so long looked inward in its economic policies and lagged well behind neighboring countries in its economic growth, has gradually since the death of Mao Zedong turned dramatically outward toward the rest of the world. As a result of radical economic policy changes, agricultural production has increased rapidly and industrial production is following suit. The PRC has discovered that the market mechanism, for all the economic and social confusion it creates, does indeed stimulate production: China's GNP growth rates have been estimated in real terms at 12.0 percent in 1984, 10.0 percent in 1985, and 9.1 percent in 1986. Meanwhile, China's debt has assumed serious dimensions—$20 billion in 1985, and $26 billion by 1987.

Even North Korea, considered by some to be the most seclusive country in the world, has announced a policy of expansion of its economic and technological ties with foreign countries. When this change was first reported in September 1984, it was proclaimed to be a step toward an open economic policy, and by 1987 there were increasing signs that such a policy was emerging.

The economic future, therefore, looks bright in the entire Asian-Pacific region, and especially in Northeast Asia. What political-military structure supports these bright prospects, and what are its basic components? First, the United States and the Soviet Union today maintain the military balance in the region, and neither superpower seems to want to bring about a drastic change in the status quo. For the United States at least, drastic change could bring serious results. For example, if American military power were to diminish significantly in the region, North Korea might revert to its goal of military unification of the Korean Peninsula and draw back from its avowal of an open-door policy. Or if the Japanese public were to perceive the United States to be militarily far weaker than the Soviet Union, it might grow critical of the Japan-U.S. alliance, and urge a policy of greater submissiveness to the Soviet Union.

The second positive factor contributing to economic development in Northeast Asia is the post World War II emergence of what I call the system for encapsulating local conflicts. In the contemporary society of nations, a close political and military linkage exists between local systems and the global system: a local conflict produces an immediate global impact. Nevertheless, a fairly effective deterrent has evolved to contain conflicts when they erupt and to limit their disruptive consequences. We have, in other words, by dint of the strong global-regional linkage, a system encapsulating conflict. Consider, for example, Hungary in 1956, the Sino-Indian War of 1962, Czechoslovakia in 1968, four Middle East wars, the Sino-Soviet border clashes of 1969, Angola in 1976, Ethiopia in 1978, Kampuchea in 1979 and Afghanistan in 1979. All instances of encapsulated conflicts, none of these escalated into large-scale general war. True, in every case impacts were felt throughout the international system, but economic activities outside the areas of conflict were not directly hindered.

Even the Korean War and the Vietnam War were successfully encapsulated; otherwise either one might well have escalated into the unthinkable: World War in a nuclear era. In both cases impacts on the international society were significant and both proved to be turning points in world history. But neither war hindered economic activities in other areas.

TOWARD FURTHER STABILITY IN EAST ASIA

Five conditions are necessary for improved stability in Northeast Asia: stable Japan-U.S. relations, stable Sino-American relations, stable Sino-Japanese relations, stable Sino-Soviet relations, and the encapsulation of regional conflicts.

First, as for Japan-U.S. relations, trade frictions between the two countries continue, with the import barriers set up by the Japanese government still one source of major concern in the United States. It appears, however, that the overall economic picture has begun to change for the better: on the foreign exchange markets, the *yen* has advanced 83 percent against the U.S. dollar since 1985, but lately the dollar gained strength and the American automobile industry is showing signs of recovery. In view of such positive trends, it seems reasonable to expect that economic problems between the United States and Japan can be resolved one after another without serious damage to the political and military bonds between these nations.

Second, Sino-American relations have encountered many problems since the inauguration of President Ronald Reagan, yet persuasion and negotiation between the two governments have persisted because neither side wants to nullify the progress already made. The tragic events in Beijing in June 1989, however, worsened the Sino-American relations. Nevertheless, President George Bush opted against dismantling of a constructive U.S.-Chinese relationship, built up so carefully over two decades.

Taiwan, of course, is a major focus for dispute between the United States and the PRC. When the U.S. government announced a plan to export military equipment worth $760 million to Taiwan in March 1984, Beijing immediately denounced the move as a violation of the Sino-American joint communiqué of August 17, 1982. In June 1984, a spokesman for the Chinese Ministry of Foreign Affairs protested a U.S. decision to sell C-130 military transport aircraft to Taiwan, and in October of that year, Deng Xiaoping expressed his concern about Sino-American relations when he told visitors from the Japanese Komeito (Clean Government Party), "A mistake in handling the Taiwan issue could bring about a catastrophe in Sino-American relations."

However, military exchange between the two countries has been increasing, especially since June 1983, when the U.S. government announced a relaxation of regulations on the export of advanced technology to the People's Republic of China. A group of four Chinese military officers, headed by the son of Defense Minister Zhang Aiping, visited the United States in February 1984 to explore the possibility of Sino-American cooperation with regard to air defense systems and anti-tank systems. In June, Minister Zhang himself visited the United States, received a warm welcome in Washington, and departed amid reports that both sides had agreed to closer military cooperation. In October, an American military group visited China to observe military exercises, and in January 1985 a group of American logistics experts visited China. China now accepts port-calls of American warships so long as they remain strictly diplomatic courtesy calls. The two governments' agreements on the transfer of some U.S. military technology to the PRC however, was suspended by the American side following the June 1989 Chinese crackdown on pro-democracy demonstrators in Beijing.

The honeymoon between China and Japan meanwhile seems to have ended, too, with China euphoria no longer much in evidence in Japan. Nevertheless, as long as economic growth remains China's foremost national goal, Japan will continue to be China's most useful and powerful neighbor by virtue of its ample capital and technology. China, on the other hand, remains an attractive neighbor for Japan owing to the vast consumer market and source of cheap labor inherent in its one billion population. Reflecting upon the lessons of history between these two nations, leaders on both sides are now convinced that the interests of both are best served by continuing friendly ties. This view seems unlikely to change so long as China's first priority is economic growth.

Political relations between Tokyo and Beijing also have progressed. In November 1983; Hu Yaobang, then General Secretary of the Chinese Communist Party, visited Japan; the following March, Prime Minister Nakasone made a return visit. Since then, the foreign ministers of both countries, Abe Shintaro of Japan and Wu Xuequan of China, have met three times. Relations with China were clouded by a Japanese court decision in February 1987 recognizing the right of Taiwan to maintain possession of a Chinese student dormitory in Kyoto. The incident was settled through diplomatic negotiations. The June 1989 events in China understandably disturbed Japan, but overall normal relations were maintained.

Progress in military exchange likewise should be noted. In July 1984, on his way back from the United States, Chinese Defense Minister Zhang Aiping met with Japanese Defense Director General Kurihara Yuko. In the spring of 1985, Natsume Haruo, Japanese Defense Vice-Minister, visited China and was well received. Since then, the exchange of persons and information has been increasing quietly but steadily.

First-phase construction on the Baoshan steel plant, which was much criticized in China as well as Japan, is finally complete. The plant is now producing coke, pig iron, and steel.

Japan's exports to China in 1986 stood at over $9 billion, a 47-percent increase over the previous two years; Japan's imports from China in the same year were nearly $6 billion. The total Sino-Japanese trade figure of some $15 billion for that year represented roughly a quarter of China's entire international trade. It is indicative that by 1986, Japan became China's largest trading partner and the two countries' economic ties are maintained.

It is in Sino-Soviet relations that the world has observed the most radical changes in the Far East in the 1980s. The Tashkent appeal to China extended by Leonid Brezhnev in March 1982 brought a major turning point in Sino-Soviet relations. Prior to the Tashkent speech, relations between the two countries had long been severely strained. Indeed, in its 1975 Constitution China defined the Soviet Union as a "socialist imperialist," and thereafter Chinese leaders regularly denounced the Soviet hegemonism. However, China's unexpectedly affirmative reaction to the Tashkent speech came about in response to Chinese uneasiness about Reagan's policies toward Taiwan. The result was a reopening of the long suspended Sino-Soviet talks at the foreign vice-minister level, in October 1982. Chinese authorities expressed sincere condolences at Brezhnev's funeral later in the year; and during the second round of talks, in March 1983, both parties agreed to encourage cultural exchange between the two nations as well as to expand Sino-Soviet trade to the level of $800 million. Thereafter, the third round of foreign vice-minister talks was held in October 1983, the fourth in March 1984, and the fifth in October 1984. And in December 1984, Soviet First Deputy Premier Ivan Arkhipov visited China, in symbolic recognition of the progress in trade relations and personnel exchanges.

But for all the progress made in relations between the PRC and the USSR, it must be remembered that China has made it clear that full normalization of relations with the Soviet Union rests on three conditions:

withdrawal of Soviet forces in Afghanistan; suspension of Soviet support for the Vietnamese invasion of Kampuchea; and general withdrawal of Soviet forces deployed on the Sino-Soviet and Sino-Mongolian borders. For reasons of their own, the Soviets evacuated their troops from Afghanistan. They have also withdrawn some of their military units from outer Mongolia and influenced Hanoi's decision to withdraw its troops from Kampuchea. Finally, in May 1989, Soviet Secretary General Mikhail Gorbachev was able to visit Beijing. Subsequently, contacts between the Soviets and the PRC have been gradually increased and political and economic relations between the two countries are progressing. Party-to-Party relation in the era of Gorbachev's presidency seems irrelevant.

Finally, the on-going regional conflicts seem at present to be satisfactorily encapsulated. The Afghan war did not spread into either Iran or Pakistan; the Kampuchean conflict does not seem to be spreading into Thailand. The international climate, therefore, does not appear to be deteriorating as a result of these conflicts.

Conflict conditions inside Northeast Asia are actually improving somewhat with the gradual resolution of certain potentially volatile issues. An agreement between China and Britain on the future of Hong Kong was reached after a series of cautious negotiations: sovereignty over Hong Kong and Kowloon, including the New Territories, will return to China in 1997. Even relations between China and Taiwan, although certainly not free from tensions, are currently fairly stable. (Long-term projections for China-Taiwan relations are discussed in detail below.)

The Korean Peninsula, long considered to be the greatest potential crisis point in Northeast Asia, is now gradually showing signs of change, despite North Korea's continued intermittent recourse to terrorism. In May 1983, when a Chinese civil airliner bound from Shenyang to Shanghai was hijacked by Chinese and landed at a South Korean airport, South Korea ignored a strong demand from Taiwan to allow the hijackers to be returned immediately to Taiwan and instead tried them in Korea before remanding them to Taiwan. On other occasions, including private-level contacts as well as indirect governmental contacts through the Japanese government, the South Korean government has shown an extremely friendly attitude toward the PRC. For example, when a revolt took place on a Chinese torpedo boat off the Korean coast in March 1985, the South Korean government handled the incident in accordance with Beijing's wishes.

Particularly conspicuous has been the development of athletic and cultural contacts between South Korea and China. In March 1984, South Korea participated in the Eastern Zone of the Davis Cup tennis tournament held in Kunming, PRC. A Chinese youth basketball team visited South Korea in April 1984. Twelve experts from Chinese sports organizations visited South Korea in September of the same year. In the following year the Chinese government announced its intention to participate in the 1988 Seoul Olympics and did so in the Summer of the same year.

Until recently, Beijing had not issued visas to South Koreans except those participating in international events. But in August 1984 it allowed a scholar of South Korean nationality to make an extensive trip in the northeast region of China. In the same year China extended earnest invitations to American scholars of South Korean descent and allowed them to observe the northeast region. It is evident that exchange of persons and indirect trade between the PRC and South Korea are gradually increasing.

Since 1984, international relations involving North Korea have been worth observing, too. In that year, Hu Yaobang, then General Secretary of the Chinese Communist Party, visited Pyongyang in May. In the same month, North Korean Labor Party Chairman Kim Il Sung arrived in Moscow by way of the Trans-Siberian Railroad on a special train. It had been 23 years since his last formal visit to the Soviet Union, in 1961. During the 1984 visit when General Secretary of the Soviet Communist Party Konstantin Chernenko denounced the U.S. military buildup, and the resurgence of militarism and revengism in Japan, Kim Il Sung did not agree and no joint communiqué was announced. Presumably Kim, having failed to obtain the consent of the Soviets concerning his own successor, decided to look for amicable relations with his capitalist neighbors. He returned to Pyongyang on July 1 after visits to seven East European countries. In the meantime, a campaign was waged in Pyongyang to praise Kim Jong Il, a son of Kim Il Sung, as the heir apparent, and in August, soon after Kim Il Sung's return from his state visits, Radio Pyongyang officially announced that Kim Jong Il's position as successor was internationally recognized.

Thereafter, North Korea declared its open-door policy and North-South dialogue began. When a flood brought devastation to South Korea in the summer of 1984, North Korea immediately offered aid and, after some political deliberation, South Korea accepted the offer. With this, the ice was finally broken and the way paved for a relaxation of North-South tensions. In November 1984, North-South economic talks were held in Panmunjom, as were preliminary talks with Red Cross representatives. Then, an incident occurred which might have destroyed the whole process: North Korean forces crossed the DMZ in hot pursuit of a Soviet defector and a gunfight ensued. But both of the Korean Peninsula governments handled the affair with flexibility and circumspection. Kim Il Sung, after a visit to Beijing in November, further promoted the open-door policy and the dialogue with the South. New North-South economic talks took place in January 1985, and a Red Cross meeting in May. Both sides agreed to resume bilateral negotiations, suspended since January 1986, but they were called off by President Kim Il Sung because of the military exercises that the South conducted routinely with U.S. forces at the beginning of 1988.

U.S. INVOLVEMENT IN TAIWAN AND KOREA

Let us now explore future scenarios for Taiwan and the Korean Peninsula, the two potential crisis points in Northeast Asia where the United States is most closely involved.

For the short term, the outlook for Taiwan's future appears bright. Its economy is remarkably prosperous, and the liberalization of its domestic market has met with amazing success. Taiwan has semi-official missions in 40 countries, including Japan and the United States, and trade relations with more than 100 countries. Therefore its independence can be said to have international support, at least for the time being. Even in its indirect trade with the PRC, estimated at U.S. $2 billion in 1988, it shows impressive strength. Moreover, Taiwan's air force holds clear command over the Taiwan strait. All these factors appear to support the Taiwanese attitude of continued confidence in themselves and in their country's independence.

For the longer term, however, we must take a closer look at the three pillars that support Taiwan as an independent political entity: command air power over the Taiwan Strait, economic prosperity, and domestic political stability. First, the combat capability of the Nationalist Government's air force depends totally on U.S. policies. If the United States should refuse to provide enough fighter planes for Taiwan to maintain its air command over the strait, the PRC almost certainly would move immediately to strengthen its Liberation Army air bases in Fujian Province in preparation for a renewal of the call for armed liberation of Taiwan that was often heard during the

Great Cultural Revolution.

Second, Taiwan's prosperous economy also depends heavily on U.S. support. Led by a further surge in exports, economic growth for the year 1988 reached 10.6 percent, with per capita income surpassing $5,000. Trade relations with the United States were crucial to this strategy since the United States served as the market for 45 percent of Taiwan's total exports. Thus it is obvious that the United States is a decisive factor in Taiwan's economy as well as its defense. Indeed, by reason of these two dependencies alone, it can be said that no matter how successful Taiwan's economic policy may be or how diligent its people, its fate rests ultimately in the hands of the United States.

The island nation's third support, its domestic political stability, is, in crucial respects, more apparent than real. Generally speaking, when political stability is brought about through true democracy, it can be flexible and resilient. Taiwan's political stability is unfortunately superficial. For the rulers of Taiwan, who are mostly mainland-born, it is hard to discard this relatively easy approach to ostensible stability. The present system, however, has weak points that would not exist in a more open democracy. One weakness is bitterness and discontent among the governed, particularly among the native-born Taiwanese, a situation that is likely to continue. Another is the fact that, by American lights, the political oppression in Taiwan is still quite severe. Hence the following dilemma: again, if Taiwan wants to remain an independent state it needs strong U.S. support, which in turn depends heavily on American public opinion. To ensure the American people's sympathetic support, Taiwan must try to make its domestic administration more flexible and responsive to the popular will. If the Nationalist government neglects this effort, it may sooner or later lose U.S support no matter how prosperous its economy. And in that event, the Japanese government would no doubt fall in with the United States and turn away as well. It seems to me that leaders in the Nationalist government and in the Kuomintang party must be keenly aware of these possibilities, and that is why we are seeing some changes toward greater democratization. Let us hope these changes will not be too slight or too long in coming.

Elsewhere on the international scene, it is important to remember that South Korea, the most trustworthy Asian friend of Taiwan, is now courting Beijing while Taiwan continues its policy of no contacts, no negotiations and no concessions vis-à-vis the PRC. Here is but one more sign of Taiwan's growing isolation in the world. The Kuomintang government cannot afford to assume that 40 years in power in any way secures its continued survival; the nation needs creative but careful change of policy if it is to enjoy long-term independence and prosperity. One new alternative, an alternative involving elements of danger to be sure, would be for Taiwan to explore a framework of peaceful coexistence with Beijing while it still has negotiating power.

Another potential crisis point in Asia, the Korean Peninsula, seems gradually but certainly headed for a relaxation of tensions. In this scenario, the decision of the International Olympic Committee's (IOC) to hold the 1988 Olympics in Seoul stand out as a turning point. The Chinese intention of participating was announced quickly after the decision of the IOC; participation of the Soviet Union and East European countries followed. At the beginning, North Korea wanted the Soviet Union and other socialist countries to boycott the Seoul Olympics; North Korea demanded a co-sponsorship with South Korea and then instituted a terrorist attack on a Korean airliner so that people would be afraid to go to South Korea. All these efforts were in vain.

Some time ago, North Korean leaders set forth three strategies for possible unification of the Korean Peninsula: (1) formal, generalized military actions of the kind conducted in the Korean War in 1950; (2) localized, intermittent guerilla and terrorist activities aimed at disrupting the economy and security of South Korea; and (3) political harassment designed to take advantage of internal political problems in South Korea. Currently, none of these options holds much promise as a practical means of reunification, and leaders in Pyongyang must have already conceded this point (at any rate, they have doubtless learned that adventurous actions such as those conducted in Rangoon and Bahrain can produce numerous adverse effects and increase their international isolation). The only alternative left to them is to coexist and compete peacefully with South Korea. The PRC has long urged this policy for North Korea, and so now does the Soviet Union, albeit more tentatively.

Therefore, we can safely assume that North Korea's current open-door policy and its apparently flexible posture toward the South will continue for some time to come. There is a view that Kim Jong Il is better informed and more knowledgeable than his father about the world situation and attaches greater importance to economic development. Indeed, another view attributes the relaxation of seclusiveness and the diminution of guerrilla and terrorist activities directly to Kim Jong Il's influence. All these projections support a scenario of continuing North Korean flexibility and permit the possibility that cross-recognition between the two governments may become a reality. If relations between Seoul and Beijing become closer, if relations between Seoul and Moscow follow, and if relations between Pyongyang and Tokyo improve, then by the end of the 1980s we may find stable peaceful coexistence between the North and the South, and cross-recognition by the major four powers in the area: the People's Republic of China, the Soviet Union, Japan, and the United States.

THE FOUR POWERS RELATIONSHIP

With respect to Sino-American relations, we have already singled out Taiwan as the stumbling block in the road to improved relations. Experiences in 1983 and 1984 have shown us that if the United States ignores Beijing's perspectives concerning the Taiwan question and conspicuously favors the Nationalist position, Beijing will feel cornered and will retaliate by resisting U.S. overtures to improve Sino-American relations. In fact, any PRC policy that serves to damage those relations may be taken as a token of protest. If Sino-American cooperation is to improve in Northeast Asia, then, the United States must adopt cautious policies toward Taiwan.

In this connection, it will be interesting to see how Washington makes use of the Taiwan Relations Act in reconciling its friendships with Beijing and Taipei. It is my speculation that the United States will gradually begin to assist direct negotiations between Beijing and Taipei, and that ultimately their peaceful coexistence may be realized through U.S. mediation. If U.S. policies in fact take such a course, Sino-American relations will become stable. If the Soviet Union remains the common adversary, China and the United States in this scenario will develop political, economic, and military cooperation smoothly. But the trend can be halted or altered.

As for Sino-Soviet relations, China once propagated the assertion that the Soviet Union was girding for an attack on China. So long as the Chinese believed that the Soviet Union intended what Robert Halfeman called a nuclear "surgical strike" on the Chinese nuclear plants, it made sense for them to prepare accordingly. Soviet policy toward China changed in the 1980s, however, and the Chinese analysis of Soviet affairs has become more sophisticated; no one in the PRC leadership today seriously believes that the Soviet Union intends to invade China. Therefore, the Chinese are making radical personnel reductions in the People's Liberation Army, and underground nuclear shelters are now considered useless.

Mikhail Gorbachev's May 1989 visit to Beijing improved Sino-Soviet relations. I am, however, convinced that for China, at the moment, the West holds far greater allure than the USSR, and for one obvious reason. Over the last decade China has had many opportunities to compare Soviet and Western science and technologies. Their conclusion is inescapable. The Boeing 747 is superior to any Ilyushin jet in every possible respect. Ford and Toyota trucks are better built than their Soviet counterparts. A Volga or a Moscovich is no match for a Toyota or a Nissan. IBM computers are still number one in the world, and the United States is far ahead of all others in computer software development. As long as economic development remains China's prime national goal, a revival of strength in the Sino-Soviet alliance akin to that of the 1950s is unthinkable for the near future. However, the two nations are equally unlikely to find it necessary to go back to the strained relations before 1976. In other words, Sino-Soviet relations will change only at a slow pace unless the nature of leadership in each country undergoes a radical transformation.

The question then arises: Is a change of political leadership in the PRC likely to come about? To answer this, we must examine the current socioeconomic situation in China, which has as perhaps its most important feature an exploding popular demand for consumer goods. Both agriculture and industry are currently geared to this demand, and the adoption of a marketing mechanism is making rapid production growth possible. For example, China produced six million electric washing machines in 1985. Compare this figure with the Soviet Union's and Italy's four million each, and five million each for the United States and Japan in the same year. China is now the world's largest producer of electric washers.

If this response to consumer demand were to be halted and a policy of asceticism imposed, a great deal of leadership power would be required. Can a leadership with such power emerge in today's China? Though fluctuation between liberalization and rectification may take place, as happened following the June 1989 events in Beijing, the resurgence of puristic radicalism and of the "politics-takes-command" principal that prevailed during the Cultural Revolution seems only temporary today. In this sense, China has finally awakened after hundreds of years of dreaming since Marco Polo envisioned the affluent Celestial Empire. Politically, Japanese-American relations are closer and more cooperative than ever.

But economically serious frictions exist and are likely to continue. Friction-free relations between any two highly competitive industrialized countries are all but impossible. The main future task of Japanese and Americans will focus on recognizing that reality and working out constructive ways of dealing with it. Currently, the Japanese government is reinforcing its efforts to reduce economic frictions, and the Bush administration is taking cautious steps to reduce public ill will and to prevent unnecessary escalation of friction.

It seems certain, however, that new sources of economic competition will continue to emerge, and that as they do, they will reinforce American pressures on Japan to increase its defense expenditure, hence to improve its defense capability. Even now the Japanese government, unable to deny all American requests and suggestions, is gradually increasing its defense budget and military cooperation with the United States. A too rapid increase of Japanese defense expenditure and military capability would certainly arouse suspicion in North Korea, South Korea, the ASEAN countries and the PRC, but too little would just as certainly exacerbate political problems between Japan and the United States. The only alternative left to Japan and the United States seems to be a middle course toward military cooperation developing at a moderate speed.

No great obstacles exist in current relations between Japan and the People's Republic. Economic ties between the two countries will doubtless become closer and closer in the future. However, I suspect that cultural frictions will develop as people-to-people contacts increase.

The Chinese, historically so used to occupying the center of civilization in the East, are a proud and even ethnocentric people; the Japanese, less centrally located and more accustomed to accommodating other civilizations, have long ago developed what I call a "peripheral minority complex." Those with a peripheral minority complex are prone to deal in a somewhat inferior fashion with those at the center of civilization. When they in fact find themselves in an inferior power position, they tend to become overly submissive and try hard to learn from the center. At the same time, however, they develop a strong sense of rivalry driven by a will to excel. Once they are convinced they have surpassed the center and have become stronger, they trend to become aggressive and arrogant toward their erstwhile superiors. They are not given to balanced relationships between equals.

How might today's Japan, with its superior technology and abundant capital, conduct its relations with China? The Japanese of course feel superior to the Chinese now, in terms of technological advancement and capital accumulation, and they may act accordingly. The proud Chinese would never accept such Japanese attitudes. One way in which the Chinese might try to counter the effect would be to exploit the kind of guilt-complex thinking developed by Japanese intellectuals since the defeat of Japan. Here in this psychological dimension, I suspect, resides the largest stumbling block in Sino-Japanese relations.

4

Economic Development Strategy of China for the 1990s and Beyond
Qian Yongnian

As the weight of world economic and political power shifts increasingly to the Pacific, interactions among three of the Pacific countries—China, Japan, and the United States—no doubt will produce impacts that are important not only for the countries named but for the whole world as well. Therefore, these interactions and their implications as well as a Chinese perspective on China's economic development strategy for the 1990s and beyond are indeed worthy of study. Hopefully it will provide some clues to facilitate an improved general understanding of China's development aims and, by extension, an appreciation of the world impacts implied.

In terms of economic growth, the People's Republic of China, has made much progress since its founding in 1949. It has established a fairly comprehensive industrial system and a national defense adequate to uphold its sovereignty and independence. With only 7 percent of the world's arable land, China has succeeded in feeding and clothing about 22 percent of the world's population, and the persistent starvation and cyclical famines so long associated with the old China have been virtually eliminated. China now leads the world in total agricultural output value and ranks among the leading growers of grain, cotton, and produce. Its industrial output value now ranks fifth in the world, and it is a major producer of coal, steel, cement and electricity. Moreover, China has made promising strides in the development of high technology.

On the other hand, China has not been entirely successful in its development endeavors, owing in part to impractical policies and in part to an excessively centralized and inflexible economic management system. What is more, the chaos of the ten-year "Cultural Revolution" hindered economic growth and served to widen the economic gap between China and other countries, so that in terms of per capita GNP, China still lags far behind the developed countries.

In 1978, in an effort to speed up the nation's economic growth, China's leadership introduced sweeping reforms to restructure the economy. These reforms released tremendous productivity. In the past decade, China has roughly doubled its GNP, its national income, and its government revenues. During the 1978-1987 period, China's GNP registered an annual growth rate about 10 percent higher than that of most of the countries in the world. In 1987, China's GNP reached one trillion, 92 billion Chinese yuan, a 9.4 percent increase over the year before, and its industrial and agricultural output values registered increases of 16.5 percent and 4.7 percent respectively. As reform has deepened, Chinese policy makers, economic planners, and the general public have gradually arrived at a consensus about what path China should take in order to promote its economic development. The Thirteenth National Congress of the Communist Party of China convened in October and November of 1987. Its decisions have far-reaching effects on all aspects China's development. The Party Congress of 1987 cast into theory the general current consensus regarding the stage of development in which China finds itself and, on the basis of this articulation, a strategy for future development was mapped out.

It is generally recognized that China today is at the primary stage of socialism, a stage characterized by a low level of productivity. Out of a population of more than one billion, 800 million people live in rural areas and, for the most part, still use hand tools to make a living. A certain number of modern industries coexist with many industries that lag several decades or even a century behind present-day standards in other countries. Some areas that are fairly well developed economically coexist with vast areas that are underdeveloped and impoverished. The overall level of scientific and technological development is low. Only minimal socialization of production has been achieved, and the commodity economy and the domestic market are only beginning to develop. Given this state of relative backwardness, China's full modernization can be accomplished only over a long period, specifically a period calculated to last at least 100 years starting from 1956 (when China formally entered the stage of socialism after the founding and consolidation of the People's Republic in 1949). As these national conditions are unique to China, a developing socialist country, it cannot mechanically follow the development process of any other country. Rather, it must blaze its own trail in an effort to build a socialism grounded in Chinese characteristics. It is with these basic features of the Chinese society in mind that the Chinese government has formulated its development strategy for the years to come.

To turn China into a modern socialist country is the general goal to be pursued throughout the entire primary stage of socialism. This aim calls for transferring a predominantly agricultural country into a modern industrial-ized country and a semi-natural or natural economy into a highly developed commodity economy. Emphasis will be placed on accelerating a traditional industrial revolution while at the same time catching up with the new worldwide technological revolution.

A three-phase plan has been drawn up to achieve this development goal. The first phase, covering the 1980-1990 period, calls for a doubling of the 1980 GNP and a definitive resolution of the problem of feeding and clothing the one billion and more Chinese people. The GNP target for this phase has been met three years ahead of schedule and, as we have seen, the feeding and clothing requirement is basically satisfied. In addition, efforts are being intensified to create an economic and social environment conducive to further growth. The second phase, covering the period 1990-2000, has as its target a fourfold increase of the 1980 GNP, which would enable the Chinese people to lead a genuinely comfortable life. During the third phase, which is estimated to last from the years 2000 to 2050, China hopes to attain the average per capita GNP level of moderately developed countries elsewhere in the world.

The most important task facing the Chinese people now is to address the development goal laid out for the second phase. However, in pursuit of this goal China is faced with a number of growth constraints: inadequate resources to ensure long-term support for its large population, lack of development funds and, above all, a system of economic management that results in low economic returns. To overcome all these difficulties, it is imperative that China gradually shift its emphasis from extensive manage-ment to intensive management. Specifically, priority must be given to the following development endeavors:

1) To expand scientific, technological and educational undertakings. China's economy is characterized by a consumption of exhaustible resources that simply cannot be sustained on a long-term basis. Therefore, major efforts will be made to modernize the technology and equipment of such key industries as energy, raw and semi-finished materials, transport, communica-tions and machine building. This modernization will be achieved through intensified scientific and technological research. State appropriations for

scientific and technological research as well as for education will be increased year by year to raise the scientific, technological and educational levels that are so vital to indigenous economic development.

2)   To maintain a rough balance between total demand and total supply and to rationally adjust and reform the structure of production. A chronic and excessive blind investment fever that far exceeds the national strength but yields only poor returns has plagued the Chinese economy for years, resulting in a tremendous waste of resources. This investment fever must be brought under control. At the same time, industry must be restructured, with emphasis on the development infrastructure and consumer industries, through the use of economic levers such as price, taxation, and credit to achieve an optimal distribution and utilization of resources.

3)   To increase agricultural productivity. Although China's agricultural growth has been quite remarkable, agriculture remains a weak section in the economy because production is still unsteady. To ensure a constant supply of grain sufficient to feed China's vast and burgeoning population, the Chinese government has decided to increase its input into agriculture substantially. Supplies of chemical fertilizer and farm machinery will be increased and farm credits will be expanded. The practice of contracting farmland to peasant households, a proven incentive for increasing farm production, will continue. Where conditions are favorable, peasants will be encouraged to cooperate in commercialized farming ventures on a voluntary and equal basis and to gradually expand the scale of such ventures. Meanwhile, the growth of rural industries will receive sizable support, both as a means of absorbing the millions of rural laborers freed from agriculture by modernized farming methods and as a means of generating funds to sustain and increase agricultural production.

4)   To expand China's economic relations with the outside world. Opening-up, one of the most important strategic decisions adopted by the present government, was instituted a decade ago to boost China's economy. During the ensuing ten years, China used 33 billion dollars in foreign loans and investment and set up close to 9,000 Sino-foreign joint ventures in China. It also set up four special economic zones and opened fourteen coastal cities to absorb foreign investment and capital. The same open policy that has proved so instrumental in promoting China's economic growth so far will be pursued with added vigor in the years to come. The reason is clear: China has an acute shortage of development funds, but it also has a vast, inexpensive, and disciplined labor force concentrated in the

coastal areas. Indeed, to address the shortage and utilize the labor advantage, the Chinese government recently decided to encourage the whole coastal area, embracing a population of some 200 million, to participate fully in international commodity production and exchange. With this policy in force, the economy of the coastal area will become externally oriented, characterized by massive imports of raw materials to be processed for re-export. Hainan Island, which is slightly smaller than Taiwan, will soon become a province with the full status of a special economic zone.

In addition, new incentives will be offered to foreign investors. Leaders of the Chinese Communist Party, stressed that China welcomes foreign business investment in the coastal areas. To this end, China not only should encourage more wholly foreign-owned enterprises to operate on China soil, but also should allow foreign business to manage or play a dominant role in the management of more Sino-foreign joint ventures and cooperative enterprises. With all these changes, China will soon be seen as an aggressive presence on the international economic scene. What is more, it is expected that the accelerated economic growth of the coastal region will in turn assist the flow of capital into the less developed interior and thus spur growth nationwide.

The greatest obstacle China has faced in its development drive is an economic structure that has become increasingly incompatible with the goal of sustained economic growth. The experiences of the past decade have proved that reform of this economic structure is absolutely essential in the promotion of China's economic growth. Similarly, the success of China's strategy for future economic development depends on an accelerated and intensified reform of the economic structure.

China's economic reform began in 1978 in the rural areas and brought major progress before the focus shifted in 1984 to the urban areas, where it is now in full swing. Steadily, as the reform has proceeded, a new economic structure has evolved to supersede the existing one so that today the reform taking place in China is properly regarded as a second revolution because of its profound impact both in conceptual thinking and in practice.

First, among the several important principles that have been evolved to guide the current reform is the one that says China should strive to develop a commodity economy that integrates socialist planning with market supply and demand. This represents a radical rupture with past dogma, which held that a commodity economy is alien to socialism. According to the current formulation, planning should be conducted according to the principle of commodity exchange and the law of value. The state should regulate the market, and the market should guide enterprise. Specifically, this means that the state regulates the relation between supply and demand through economic, legal, and administrative means, and thereby creates a favorable economic and social environment for sound enterprise management decisions. Under the guidance of this general principle, China expects to establish over time the basic framework for a planned commodity economy.

Second, a central task of China's current economic reform is to invigorate publicly owned enterprises by separating ownership from management so as to make managers fully responsible for their own decisions and for the profits and losses that result. In future the management of enterprises will be contracted or leased to those who qualify through a competitive bidding process. Those businesses which fare badly can no longer expect government subsidies. If they cannot survive the competition, they will either go bankrupt or be taken over by new management. As a matter of fact, this process has already occurred in a number of enterprises.

Third, an open and competitive socialist market system will be set up to promote commodity exchange. A financial market will be set up for the issue and exchange of stocks and bonds to pool and distribute the capital needed for production. Similarly, the labor market, the technology market, and the real estate market will be opened to competition to facilitate economic growth. The general position is that China is ready to adopt all the economic mechanisms essential to the functioning of a modern commodity economy.

Fourth, the pricing system, which heretofore has distorted and consequently failed to reflect the supply-demand relationship, will be gradually and prudently reformed. The state will control the price of a few vital commodities and services while leaving the great majority to be regulated by the market.

Fifth, the macro-economic control system based mainly on indirect control will be extended. Henceforth the government will regulate the economy mainly by economic leverage while gradually disengaging itself from direct management. In the past, government control over the economy was total and absolute. Thanks to the reform, such control now has been reduced to cover only 50 percent of the economy, and it will be further reduced to cover only 30 percent.

Sixth, while public ownership will continue to dominate the basic means of production, the Chinese government now also encourages the growth of individual and private sectors, for practice has shown that these sectors can play a useful role in supplementing the public economy. The number of people engaged in individual and private business has jumped from 140,000 in 1978 to over 20 million. The output value of individual and private business in 1988 accounted for about 3 percent of China's total industrial output value, a modest share to be sure, but one fast increasing with government blessing. Chinese-foreign joint ventures, cooperative enterprises, and wholly foreign businesses are also encouraged in China. The government will protect the legitimate interests of foreign investors and improve the investment environment for them. Such a multi-ownership structure will instill vitality into China's economy.

In the history of modern China, the comprehensive reform now under way is unprecedented. China's present development strategy can be reached through these measures. It is expected that in the 1990s China's GNP will register an annual growth rate of 7.5 percent, its industrial and agricultural output will register an annual growth rate of 7.5 percent and 4 percent respectively, and the national income will show a 6.7 percent annual increase. By the end of this century, China's total industrial and agricultural output value is expected to reach 2.9 trillion yuan, which translates to about U.S. $1 trillion calculated according to the 1980 dollar-yuan exchange, or a fourfold increase over the 1980 valuation. The average per capita national income will reach U.S. $770. China was the eighth largest economy in the world in 1986 and rose to seventh place in 1987; it expects to become the world's fifth or sixth largest economy by 1990, and by then the scientific and technological gap between China and the advanced countries will be reduced to 10-20 years.

According to a report submitted in 1987 to President Ronald Reagan by the Committee on Integrated Long-term Strategy, a committee composed of such noted U.S. figures as Henry Kissinger and Zbigniew Brzezinski, China stands a good chance of becoming the second or third largest economy in the world by the year 2010. This estimate is backed by a study conducted by the Rand Corporation, which forecasts that China's GNP will grow at an annual rate of 4.6 percent until 2010.

The Chinese government certainly feels flattered by such forecasts. Its own planners tend to be rather more cautious in their productions; however, they do believe that with steady development China will surely move beyond sixth place and possibly beyond fifth in terms of economic strength. A strong and prosperous China is a goal that not only will serve the interest of the people of China but also will help maintain peace and stability in the Pacific and in the world at large.

All this sounds fine and encouraging. But will China in fact be able to press on with its reform and development efforts, or will it some day be compelled to draw back to the beaten track of the past? This question is always in the minds of those who follow developments in China, and it reflects a concern, which is understandable for anyone contemplating the enormity of China's task and the country's economic record up to a decade ago. The concern seems less necessary, however, in the light of the experiences of the past ten years, which have proved that reform is the only viable alternative for China's future development. Reform has already tremendously benefitted the one billion Chinese people, and therefore it has won their whole-hearted support. When one billion people get behind a policy in which they have a great stake, it is difficult for anyone to change it. What is more, a reliable guarantee of continuation for China's current policy was created with the convocation of the Thirteenth Party Congress, which elected a leadership deeply involved in and committed to reform. This leadership can be counted upon to guide China's reform and economic development forward.

Finally, people in China have come to realize that in the end, economic reform will not succeed without political reform. With this in mind, the Party has decided to adopt a number of measures to reduce excessive centralization of power, combat bureaucracy, and improve socialist democracy and legality. All these steps no doubt will facilitate the progress of China's economic reform and development.

This is certainly not to suggest that everything will be smooth sailing for China. The path of reform has never been a smooth one. Old habits of thinking and doing die hard and will inevitably create barriers along the way. New problems, too, will crop up from time to time. Yet China has learned from its past experiences, both positive and negative, and its leadership will not be deterred easily by obstacles, no matter what form they may take. For the Chinese people, there is only one way: they must go forward along the road to economic strength with every determination until China attains its goals.

5

Economic Growth Trends of Japan in the 1990s and Beyond: A Non-Economist's Perspective
Ronald Aqua

THE HIGH-YEN ERA

Contrary to the expectations of some stubborn skeptics, Japan has experienced a fundamental shift in the structure of its economy toward the kind of consumption-led growth recommended by the Maekawa Report several years ago. Statistics confirm that 1987 was a watershed year for Japan; in this year exports shrank, imports from nearly all quarters advanced sharply (except, regrettably, from the United States), and domestic demand for such basics as better quality housing soared.

The global imbalances that were driven in no small measure by a seemingly unstoppable Japanese export machine had finally begun to moderate. With the advent of the cheap dollar and a concomitant shift in the terms of trade, Japanese consumers confounded the skeptics by showing a strong inclination to purchase German cars, Taiwanese televisions, and Korean VCRs. Only time will tell whether this new spending binge will reflect itself on the household savings side as well.

The major Japanese companies, however, remained extremely competitive in global markets, thanks to single-minded efforts to retain market share in such critical sectors as automobiles and consumer electronics. At the same time, they began efforts at a fundamental overhaul of corporate strategies, anticipating the day when present markets for their exports would be saturated with high-quality products originating in the lower-wage economies of Southeast Asia and even Latin America. After the overhaul they doubtless will place much greater emphasis on knowledge-intensive industries, and the trend toward offshore operations no doubt will accelerate. These changes are likely to draw into the international trade scene ever greater numbers of "second tier" Japanese industries, such as parts and components manufacturers, that previously were satisfied to concentrate on domestic markets.

Japanese exporters have defied conventional economic thinking by their ability through successive cost-trimming to remain competitive in sectors where the yen appreciation should long since have driven them from international markets. Western economists have had to rethink the assumptions behind their "J-curve" theories, and would-be competitors have learned the hard way not to write the Japanese off too quickly.

As we enter the last decade of this century, Japan can look with some confidence toward moderate consumption-led growth and relative price stability (barring unforeseen developments such as a sudden destabilization of oil prices). It also faces the happy prospect of virtual full employment; indeed, a national debate has begun on the need to import "guest workers" to fill many of the low-end jobs, such as unskilled factory and restaurant work, that no longer attract Japanese applicants.

But there are limits, even for the indefatigable Japanese.

If Japan is to absorb foreign workers at home and successfully integrate them at every level into its growing number of operations abroad, it must devise effective strategies to break down traditional Japanese inhibitions against cross-cultural communication. This type of adjustment will be infinitely more difficult to engineer than, say, coping with a rapidly appreciating yen, involving as it does basic attitudes and value systems.

The Japanese are also justifiably concerned about the ability of their educational system to produce a citizenry that is not only competent and literate but even, with respect to the basic sciences, manifestly creative. The Japanese have been accused many times of taking a "free ride" in basic research, exploiting the inventiveness of others to churn out profitable applications. In addition, they perceive a need for change in the direction and focus of educational priorities in order to cope effectively with a world in which the production-innovation cycle is measured in weeks and months rather than years or decades.

Some other practical limitations bear mention. One is the sheer unavailability of land in the home islands for further development. Another is the rapid aging of the Japanese population, a phenomenon certain to influence savings and consumption patterns as well as the size of the labor pool and even the future course of political affairs and social policy. Yet another is the erosion of traditional familial and gender roles.

Japan no doubt will remain a society fundamentally conservative in its world view, cautious and even suspicious toward encroachment from the outside world. Thus desire for change is always likely to be tempered to some extent by faith in well-worn patterns of behavior and time-tested ways of thinking. What is more, younger Japanese are said to be less inclined than their parents to look to the West for guideposts to the future: their contribution to global affairs may have a distinctly Japanese flavor that departs distinctively from the attitudes prevalent among Japan's postwar rebuilders and consolidators.

A CHANGING GLOBAL ENVIRONMENT

From time to time Japanese leaders ponder the possibility that some day the United States will not be able to honor its global commitments, because it will find itself no longer able to manage its own structural fiscal and trade deficits. Not surprisingly, when this thought intrudes, the Japanese establishment feels moved to let Americans know of their concern and to urge remedial action.

Unfortunately from the Japanese point of view, this kind of goal has served as a catalyst, in turn, for renewed American interest in the subject of defense burden-sharing in general and of a more substantial Japanese role in particular. Sometimes in this context Americans come up with startling proposals. Recently, for example, there were suggestions that the Japanese pay cash for the protection afforded their tankers in international shipping lanes, and that they pay the rent on the large American bases in the Philippines. Although such propositions do not as a rule induce the kind of measured and thoughtful analysis in Japan that their sponsors might wish, they do help to keep alive discussions within Japan about "internationalization" and Japan's role in a changing world.

Most Japanese would rather not face up to the question of a greater political role for Japan in the world of the 1990s and beyond. They still see themselves as citizens of a relatively poor and extremely vulnerable country. For all the press reportage about Japan as the world's largest creditor nation, its move to second place (behind Switzerland and ahead of the

United States) among the richest countries in the world on a per capita
basis, and its highly visible real estate acquisitions in Hawaii, New York, and
Los Angeles, middle-class Japanese breadwinners wonder why they cannot
afford adequate housing for their families within reasonable commuting
range of their offices. And because these same breadwinners regard
themselves as already hopelessly overtaxed, they wonder how they can
possibly afford to pay yet more of their earnings toward an enhanced
Japanese military role—should the constitutional issue somehow be resolved
to legitimize such a role.

While outsiders might argue that all this protest begs the question,
given the enormous capital reserves Japan has been accumulating, politicians
in the ruling Liberal Democratic Party correctly observe that the tax issue
in particular is an extremely volatile one that could cause them great harm
if not prudently handled. And prudence, in this case, dictates adherence to
a slightly modified version of the status quo, a "revenue neutral" approach,
in our terms, that addresses only some of the most egregious inequities in
the current Japanese tax code. Beyond that, they forecast little public
tolerance for fiscal expansion on the order of magnitude that would be
required to elevate Japan to the status of even a modest global military
power.

Beyond the practical limitations imposed by normal democratic
processes, there is a psychological constraint that is rarely discussed publicly
but lurks in the minds of many Japanese. This has to do with their lack of
a well developed sense of global mission of the kind that seeks to spread
indigenous precepts for the benefit of all mankind. Historically, the
Americans, and before them the Europeans, could articulate a moral basis
for their international behavior. So could the Soviets, after their own
fashion. But most modern-day Japanese, whether because of the failure of
their postwar educational system to address the issue of international
responsibility or because of left-over guilt feelings from the dark days of
prewar militarism, or simply out of concentration on the task of economic
expansion to the exclusion of other important societal tasks, do not have
strong convictions about the shape of a future world order.

This conceptual vacuum leaves the nation vulnerable to the possibility
that one or another fringe element, of which there are many on both
extremes of the political spectrum, may manipulate public opinion in
nonconstructive ways. The recent commercial success of certain virulently
anti-Semitic publications affords but one example of this possibility. Anti-

Semitism as a cultural force is largely irrelevant in the Japanese context, but passive public acceptance in Japan of some writings that would be quickly seen as very nasty indeed in most Western societies reveals an undercurrent of alarmingly uncritical thinking about the outside world.

INTEGRATION OF THE MEGA ECONOMIES

In spite of their profound cultural differences, Japan and the United States have proved surprisingly good business partners. Both cultures embody strains of pragmatism, ambition, productivity, and efficiency that suit them well for collective ventures in many fields. As in any strong relationship, stresses and strains have developed from time to time, and no doubt these will continue to emerge. But there is a strong and growing realization on both sides that the partnership cannot afford major disruptions, and in fact over time even some deep wounds have managed to heal.

This massive and complex economic interchange has drawn the two governments into closer consultation, over a wider range of issues, than almost any other bilateral relationship in the modern world. At any given time several dozen high-level coordinative and deliberative bodies are working to reduce frictions or nurture collaboration in such fields as trade, the environment, cultural and scientific exchange, and national security. In many cases these efforts have resulted in informal policy coordination agreements between the respective executive branches, even when the national legislatures have balked at giving full support.

From the outside looking in, especially through the eyes of our NATO allies, the apparent strength of U.S.-Japanese cooperation gives rise to the haunting specter of a new "G-2," one that is distancing itself economically and technologically from the other advanced industrial countries day by day. This prospect has already had a profound psychological effect on the traditional Atlanticist players especially in the European Economic Community, who now express much uncertainty about their future role in a "G-2"-dominated world.

But the economic and political accord that has caused such consternation abroad has time and again shown itself to be extremely vulnerable to societal idiosyncrasies. This phenomenon is especially noticeable in the closely held game of national security, which seems destined increasingly to impede other economic and developmental objectives.

The so-called Toshiba Affair which surfaced in the summer of 1987 revealed an embarrassingly thin veneer of binationality covering the conduct of security affairs. As the Japanese public watched while images of American Congressmen symbolically bashing a Toshiba radio flickered on their television screens, Americans saw senior Toshiba executives tendering their resignations in what looked like a clear admission of dirty dealing. For those who had championed "quiet diplomacy" and could cite in its support some notable gains in, for example, operational-level planning between the two defense establishments, the glare of publicity revealed a startling lack of political support for such arrangements. Many defense technocrats found their plans at least temporarily stymied, and not a few Japanese regarded the American backlash as a stunning confirmation of the "Pearl Harbor syndrome" of a basic distrust between the two societies.

In the years ahead, with the American federal budget under stress, the pressure for a greater Japanese role in our mutual security will continue unabated. At the same time, resurgent economic nationalism is likely to cast a shadow over the best achievements of our economic partnership and to lend audience to those Americans who warn that the Japanese have not been especially reliable as economic partners and they might be no more reliable as security partners. From this camp we are certain to hear demands that the Japanese contribution to mutual security be made on U.S. terms and under the rubric of American strategic doctrine.

It is precisely in the area of perceived national strategic interest that the United States and Japan are most likely to clash sharply enough to dispel all notions of a "new G-2." Preliminary evidence suggests that the Japanese approach to security planning will be grounded as much in concerns for economic growth and political stability as in development of sophisticated new weapons systems. For example, to the extent that the Japanese show willingness to collaborate with the United States on foreign aid (ODA) programs, they can reliably be expected to emphasize strength of infrastructure in a recipient country rather than internal security, productivity and human resource development rather than pacification. They will not be as demanding as the Americans that ODA recipients take sides in a global ideological struggle; indeed, they may even show a willingness to assist groups that some Americans deem subversive.

In the completely separate domain of weapons technology transfer, the stage has been set for a fundamental clash of interests between those in the respective defense establishments who hope for a forthright exchange of the fruits of their national research efforts and those in the private sector who wish to exploit these efforts for commercial gain. We have already experienced the first few rounds of the contest in the selection and manufacture of new fighter aircraft and weapons systems, and more unpleasantness can be expected given the growing U.S. dependence on high-tech systems that draw on Japanese technology.

Up until now, the guiding assumption among American defense planners has been that, given Japan's dependence on the American nuclear shield and the large continuing American presence in the Pacific, the Japanese in the end will bow to U.S. initiatives. But this expectation may change abruptly once the Japanese begin to contribute in more substantial ways to the maintenance of the Western alliance system. Strongly held American views about Soviet intentions and capabilities in the Pacific almost certainly will be challenged, and the traditional American approach to security affairs in, for example, the Middle East or Central America, may be questioned as well.

In short, Americans may get more input from the Japanese than they bargained for, in the absence of any clear conceptual approach to security planning that cuts across the divergent strands of thought separating the two societies. This dialogue might in turn affect integrative forces already in motion between the economies of the two countries. We should not write "G-2" off, but it is by no means a sure thing.

MANY TRIANGLES, MANY INTERESTS

It is true that China, Japan, and the United States comprise some type of strategic triangle. However, it is important to note that in fact many strategic combinations can be described in the Pacific, some excluding one or more of the three named parties—United States-Japan-South Korea, China-Japan-South Korea, China-North Korea-Soviet Union, United States-Japan-Soviet Union, to name a few. Each of these complex sets of relationships is distinctively patterned and strongly affected by peculiar strands of history, and the sets are not necessarily interlocking.

Unlike Europe, where ideological boundaries are rather clearly drawn, the Pacific region presents a striking array of contending forces loosely contained within a conceptual fuzziness and strategic vagueness. While the result can hardly be called a power vacuum, it presents a situation ripe for experimentation that cuts across political boundaries. For example, China has figured out a way to trade with South Korea, and it is not inconceivable that this new relationship might some day rank in equal importance, in terms of investment and technology transfer, with China's relationships with Japan and the United States. South Korea, for its part, is now investing in such unlikely places as Vietnam and is actively courting Eastern Europe. The Japanese have embarked on a stepped-up and independent foreign aid program in the Philippines, and even North Korea is seeking joint venture partners for new hotels and golf courses.

The United States will continue to be a dominant factor in these intra-regional developments by dint of the sheer size of its economy if not the physical presence of its forward military units. There is still a great regional dependence on the American market with its ability to soak up voluminous shipments of consumer goods, and the United States is still viewed as the country of choice in which to train a rising generation of scientists, engineers, economists, and business managers.

Americans will find themselves contending with a growing regional assertiveness in many important domains, however. Japan professes to be a new center for advanced training in many fields traditionally thought to be the preserve of American universities. South Koreans have shown themselves more than ready to tackle major infrastructural projects—dams, highways, power plants—in China. The Australians are eager to replace American beef and grain shipments to Japan with their own.

Most of the peoples in the region hope for a continuing strong American presence, but the signs of diminished U.S. influence are visible everywhere. The Chinese cannot hope to be an equal partner, in either economic or military terms, for many years to come. The Japanese may already have surpassed the United States economically, although psychologically they are not as yet disposed to a power-sharing arrangement. The Chinese and the Japanese will continue to play out their own games, as will the Chinese and the Koreans and the Japanese and the Koreans. Americans simply are not party to these cultural maneuvers, although the stakes in terms of U.S. relations with all these players are enormous.

Perhaps happily for the United States, the Soviet Union continues to blunder in its relationships in the region. Preoccupation with domestic revitalization, insensitive diplomacy, and technological backwardness have combined to deny the Soviets any significant political leverage, and even Gorbachev so far seems unable to overcome this inertia.

With the declining significance of the "Soviet threat" as a factor stimulating U.S.-Japan or U.S.-China security collaboration, the future course of any triangular defense relationship seems unclear at best. Of course, the North Koreans might decide to embark on another hostile adventure, or communists might gain the upper hand in some important province of the Philippines and thereby serve to destabilize other parts of the region. But for the moment there is clearly a desire throughout the Pacific to focus on bread-and-butter development issues and to avoid polarization along East-West or North-South lines. Somehow, the existing amorphous structure has served the region extremely well in recent years, and it seems likely that it will continue to do so well into the 1990s.

6

A Comprehensive Economic-Security Understanding of a Future PRC-USA-Japan Triangular Relationship
Hua Di

Chinese leaders usually classify international problems into two categories. In one category they consider problems of war and peace, or conflicts between East and West. In the other they consider problems of socio-economic development, or so-called North-South issues. However, this dichotomization is misleading, economy and security are interwoven and therefore must be analyzed together. Actually, the goal of a nation in making defense outlays is to buy a favorable international environment for the development of its own economy. A too expensive defense is economically counter productive and therefore contradictory to the primary goal of enhancing domestic economic prosperity and political stability. Conceived separately, national defense strategy and economic development strategy can be strategies in but a narrow sense. Only by integrating them in a consistent and harmonious combination may we arrive at what is sometimes called a comprehensive security strategy or, more aptly, a grand strategy capable of meeting both economic and security requirements for a nation in the most effective and efficient way.

It would seem that the world as a whole is moving toward a more prosperous future, because socio-economic expansion comes about through an evolution process independent of anybody's will. It is a problem, however, to discern the right path to get to that future. What will it be? A safe, economical, peaceful transition? A precarious and expensive peace bought at the price of a frenzied arms race and a terrible mutual deterrence? Or even a destructive and tragic war? One thing is obvious: the peace we have so far preserved is too expensive. Strategists and futurists are morally obligated to seek less costly and more assuredly peaceful ways to future prosperity. In the process, they must be able to present to policy decision-makers some original ideas and some logically reasoned arguments.

The line of thinking presented in this paper provides an optimistic but not totally unrealistic plan by which the PRC, the USA and Japan might strive toward the prosperity of the next century.

ECONOMIC COMPLEMENTARITY

Looking at the economic spectrum posed by five major states in the northern Pacific (PRC, USA, USSR, Japan and Canada), we may note a sharply unbalanced "North-South" polarity. On the one extreme are four well developed industrial powers, among them the world's three largest economies. On the other is China, now labeled a "Third World developing country" but by all standards a giant in terms of population: when China's population reaches its projected peak in the twenty-first century, it will be twice the size of the four other nations combined. In the narrower framework of a PRC-USA-Japan (PUJ) triangle, we can distinguish an even greater contrast in terms of economic development. The United States and Japan are well embarked upon the post-industrial or information society stage of development, with a focus on technology- and intelligence-intensive industries, or so-called third-wave industries. China is still striving mainly to build up the capital- and labor-intensive industrial infrastructures characteristic of so-called second-wave development, including an energy supply network (hydro, thermal, and nuclear power plants and power transmission systems, oil and gas fields and pipelines), a transportation network (highways, railways, waterways, and associated vehicles and facilities), and a communications network (telephone and telecommunication facilities).

From time to time one hears suggestions that China ought to bypass the second-wave stage of industrialization revolution and march straight into the modern information society; for instance Alvin Toffler, author of *The Third Wave*, made that recommendation during his visit to China in 1983. This "cut corners and follow the fashion" theory is ill founded. A simple example will serve to illustrate the inefficiency of high tech without sufficient infrastructure support. In recent years China has introduced a lot of computers in the hope of modernizing its hotel, airline and railway services. However, none of the travel agencies in Beijing today readily arrange quick reservations, rescheduling, or cancellations for a tourist who wishes to travel around China. The telephone cable network does not have enough capacity to connect the computer terminals of various hotels, ticket offices and travel agencies in Beijing alone, much less to connect computers nationwide. A clerk in a travel agency must make local and long-distance calls hotel by hotel and ticket office by ticket office and often finds all telephone lines in use. It is not unusual for a travel agent, seated in front of a computer terminal, which cannot provide information *from outside of the building* for lack of a city-wide and nation-wide communications network, to spend a whole day and still not serve a single foreign tourist and still fail to produce satisfactory results. This scenario shows that computers alone do not achieve computerization. Without a well developed communications network, the more computers bought, the more money wasted.

Broad-scale second-wave development is a prerequisite to the information revolution. The service sector cannot survive without a well developed primary industrial manufacturing sector. Generally speaking, the third-wave industries cannot substitute for second-wave industries, just as the latter could not replace agriculture as a foundation for economic development. An economy can fully enjoy high-tech high efficiency only when it operates on a strong infrastructural basis.

Not having completely achieved a traditional industrial revolution, China now finds itself particularly lacking in its transportation, communication and energy infrastructures. Like a tardy student, it must make up the half-finished course completed decades ago by today's advanced countries. This is not to say that China should foreswear all advanced technology until it has all its infrastructures in place, nor does it mean that China should build up its second-wave industries with obsolete technology. Rather, it means that China must make efforts to establish a solid foundation of traditional[1] infrastructures with advanced technology *built in*. It means, then, China must study two courses concurrently and in combination: a classic course, and a contemporary course which not only has dimensions of its own but also serves to modernize the classic course. Or to change the metaphor, we might say China must try to win two battles in one campaign.

With respect to China's current economic reform, which stresses the development of a *socialist planned commodity exchange economy*, an additional point must be noted about the significance of China's two battles. On one hand, of course, the flow of goods must be handled by means of a transportation network and the flow of information by means of a communications network. These infrastructures are indispensable to timely exchanges among producers and consumers in diverse geographic locations. On the other hand, effective and rational planning requires that a huge amount of data be quickly collected from, processed for, and fed back to all levels of the economy, and this process can best be realized through a computerized information network. Therefore, the newly defined socialist economic model is not only compatible with the concept of an advanced information society based on a strong industrial infrastructure, but it can become a reality only in such a society.

It will not be impossible for China to win the two battles simultaneously, but it will not be easy, either. Capital deficiency and shortage of time present two major difficulties, particularly with regard to infrastructure construction. For example, construction of the world famous Three Gorges hydropower project on the Yangtze River will require an investment of eight to ten billion dollars. To transmit the electricity it generates to users, several billions more will be necessary. A nuclear power plant with twin 900-megawatt reactors would cost $2.2 billion and, according to one estimate, China needs to build ten such plants in the next fifteen years, capitalization permitting. Some calculations show that, given China's terrain, the average cost of one kilometer of freeway amounts to $5 million, which is more than it would cost to purchase enough Toyota cars to cover that one-kilometer stretch. A final report on the finished construction of the Beijing-Guangzhou coaxial telephone cable indicates its cost was equal to the sum of a row of U.S. five-dollar bills lined up along the full length of the cable. Furthermore, infrastructural construction demands huge amounts and a great variety of electrical and mechanical equipment and construction materials. If China were to attempt to adhere rigidly to a closed-door policy or self-reliance, it would have to begin by creating manufacturing plants, raw material bases, and mines to ensure sufficient supplies of the requisite equipment, machines, and materials before it could start building its transportation, communication, and energy networks. However, transportation, communication, and energy in turn are necessary for the building of manufacturing plants, raw material bases, and mines. Here we have a very large circle, then. It would be possible for a self-contained economy to navigate such a circle gradually and step by step, but much time would be lost.

Most of the electrical and mechanical equipment, construction machines and materials, and civilian technology and civil engineering that China urgently needs are related to the so-called smokestack industries of the traditional manufacturing sector, and many such facilities lie idle in the United States and Japan. These post-industrial countries no longer have so many domestic sites or so much internal demand for new power plants and freeways as they had decades ago during their peak industrial development. An extensive economic cooperation in areas of infrastructural construction between developing China and developed United States and Japan could bring about enormous mutual benefits. On the Chinese side, economic development could be drastically accelerated. On the side of the United States and Japan, the benefits could be as follows:

A)   National GNP and, correspondingly, government revenues would increase;

B)   Structural unemployment could be somewhat alleviated, with decreased spending on unemployment subsidies and on re-training programs; in addition, some technical labor export might accompany the export of hardware;

C)   Economic losses due to premature depreciation of traditional industries could be reduced; this reduction would   translate to additional corporate profits and subsequently, through taxation, to increased government revenues; moreover, the "business war" between Japan and America in areas where both have surplus production capacity (e.g., steel) could be alleviated;

D)   Finally, an accelerated development of China's economy could ignite a multiplying effect on the expanding Chinese market, so that the long awaited consumer market of one billion people would no longer be out of reach to foreign business.

The complementary benefits described above, however, cannot be realized unless China has sufficient capital *in hard currency* to invest in its infrastructural construction.   A rough estimate indicates that in order to import necessary hardware and software for transportation, communication, and energy construction alone, China would need $150 billion from foreign capital resources in the next fifteen years. Where might China acquire such a huge sum of foreign capital?   There are four commonly conceivable channels: joint ventures, from the international financial market, institutional borrowing, and government loans. Unfortunately, none of these channels has worked well so far.

Foreign investors prefer to enter into joint ventures in those manufacturing and service sectors which promise quick returns in hard currency by producing goods suitable for export or by providing services for foreign tourists and business people. They are reluctant to invest in China's infrastructure construction, which requires long-term involvement and cannot yield hard currency returns. Only where a foreign exchange benefit can be assured will foreign investors be willing to put their capital into infrastructural construction. One case in point is that of the British-French investment in the Daya Bay nuclear power plant in Guangdong Province, which can sell a substantial part of its electricity to Hong Kong in exchange for hard currency. Another is the Japanese investment in a project in Shandong Province to build up the port of Shijiusuo and construct railway to the seaport; future exports of coal from the port to Japan will offset the investment. But such cases are rare. Most infrastructure construction cannot be directly export-oriented.

The international financial market is highly competitive and the cost runs high. Even at a simple interest rate as low as 8 percent, a borrowing of one billion dollars becomes a debt of $2.6 billion in twenty years. China has in fact been acquiring some capital from the commercial money market, but it cannot afford to borrow all it needs because its leaders do not want to saddle future generations with burden. Furthermore, whereas Brazil, Mexico, and other countries borrowed hundreds of billions during the years before the 1980s, the current Third World debt crisis makes it practically impossible for a late-comer like China to follow that route.

International financial institutions such as the World Bank, the International Monetary Fund, and the Asian Development Bank, have been providing long-term funds at relatively low cost for China's economic development programs. However, owing to their regulations on proportional distribution of funds, the sum available to China falls far short of its needs.

The American government, burdened with a large foreign trade deficit and an enormous national debt, does not have extra money to afford China loans on privileged or concessionary terms, even assuming that the United States is aware of, and politically willing to explore, the benefits to be gained from economic complementarity with China. Without American leadership and consent, it is unlikely that the Japanese government, which has its own financial problems, would initiate large-scale economic cooperation with China, however strategically far-sighted it may seem.

Little can be done to change the situation in the first three channels. However, there is some possibility that the impasse in the governmental channels may be broken, provided China offers something that not only is vital to the interests of the United States, Japan and other Western countries but that also can reduce their spending in some areas: something that makes them politically willing and financially able to bring about economic complementarity with China to the benefit of all three nations.

SECURITY COMPLEMENTARITY

The emerging new U.S.-Soviet detente is not going to end the world's present strategically bipolar (albeit economically multi-polar) balance. Strategic bipolarity will last long into the next century until we see a worldwide application of the PC4 concept (peaceful convergence achieved through peaceful co-existence, peaceful competition, and peaceful coopera- tion). Despite Mr. Gorbachev's announcement of new thinking in his foreign policy, the Soviet ruling body has changed neither its final political goal nor its strategy for achieving that goal. To become a patriarch in the world family remains the Soviet political goal and to edge out the United States from the old *Eurasian* continent remains the first priority in the Soviet strategy. What has changed is merely the Soviet schedule for implementa- tion of the strategy.

Inasmuch as the PRC, the USA, and Japan are all major members of the world family, a brief *global* strategic analysis must be considered in discussing a PUJ security complementarity in face of the Soviet strategy.

A Nuclear Scenario

A) Nuclear exchange between the two superpowers is of minute probability. In conditions of nuclear parity enabling with mutual assured destruction (MAD), neither superpower could benefit from a nuclear duel, which would make both outcasts from the civilized world and both losers compared with the rest of the world. However, a geostrategic *asymmetry*, whereby the USA could use forward-based conventional forces to strike heavily at the USSR by means of strategic bombing and/or ground invasion while the USSR could not retaliate in kind, makes the USSR prefer to stay with MAD rather than risk a recurrence of the World War II situation in which only the American homeland remained intact. Therefore, the strategic arms limitation talks will not result in a total elimination of all kinds of nuclear weapons, and MAD will last until *both* superpowers accept the PC4-concept.

B)   Britain, France and China can protect themselves from a Soviet nuclear bluff because even limited retaliation by any one of them could inflict enough damage on the Soviet Union to render its net strength inferior to that of the intact United States.

C)   Non-nuclear countries in NATO and the Warsaw Pact alike serve as hostages to deter both sides from using nuclear weapons: a nuclear attack on any of these hostages would invite nuclear retaliation from the opposing super power. Unfortunately, no such antithetical parity of mutual hostages exists in the cases of *Japan* and *Israel*, so that both of these nations can be used for leverage in Soviet nuclear blackmail. In the global strategic equation, even Cuba is not as important to the Soviet Union as Japan or Israel is to the United States. Therefore, *asymmetry* makes the American nuclear umbrella less than believable and the Soviet nuclear bluff credible with respect to Japan and Israel.

D)   Conventional land-based forces on both sides, whether engaged in battle or stationed at bases, also are mutual hostages, so that there is little likelihood that nuclear weapons would be used against such forces in case of a conventional showdown between the two superpowers.   However, American ships on the high seas are vulnerable to nuclear blackmail, and this because of another *asymmetry*: the Soviet Union places less defense reliance on sea-lanes than does the United States. Knowing that nuclear attacks on ships on the high seas may not escalate to nuclear attacks on ground targets, for which there are symmetries, the Soviets are most likely to use nuclear force to paralyze all sea-lanes. Therefore, in a future war, the United States could not count on the use of the sea-lanes.

To sum up, the only real danger of a major war in the future lies in a conventional showdown between two superpowers, with each sheltering itself and many other nations behind its own nuclear shield but each attempting by nuclear blackmail to exploit the opponent's "asymmetric" weak points.

A Conventional Scenario

A)   *There will be no major war in Europe.* It is not NATO's flexible nuclear response, which requires that West Europeans be willing to perish together with their eastern counterparts, that has so far deterred the Soviets from using their superior conventional forces. Rather, other negative and cost-counting considerations have made the Red Army less than eager to fight through the NATO defenses to occupy all Europe.

First, the cost to the Soviet Union of such a military conquest would include not only the cost of waging war but also the cost of reviving a ruined Europe after the conclusion of the war. The opportunity cost would be even higher. The destruction of the European economy is incompatible with the Soviet political goal of bringing a *rich* Europe into the Soviet family.

Second, the strategic gains from such a conquest would be limited. On one side, the Red Army dare not penetrate into France and Great Britain because these nations, if cornered, may resort to their own nuclear means to devastate the Soviet *homeland* and thus enhance the relative strength of the United States. On the other side, in order to dominate Eurasia, the Red Army would still have to turn eastward to deal with Japan and China.

And finally, a European campaign would place the battlefield dangerously close to the Soviet economic and political heartland. Moreover, the Kremlin knows that its allies may be dependable in defending their own soil but unreliable in a westward military adventure.

Thus, the Soviet strategic intention in Europe will be to tie down NATO conventional forces insofar as possible, and to discourage the European NATO countries from intervening in any U.S.-Soviet duel outside NATO territory.

B)   *There will be no major war in the Far East.* It would be difficult for the Red Army to sustain a large-scale protracted war in the Far East, either by means of a land invasion of China or an amphibious assault on Japan; all the territory involved is too distant from the Soviet heartland. However, for the same reason, i.e., it is distant from the heartland, the Soviet Far East is not vital to Soviet survival and neither China nor Japan and the United States can count on tying down Soviet troops there. Historically, in World War II when Japan was Hitler's former ally, one million Japanese troops in Northeast China could not tie down the Red Army when Moscow was in critical danger. It is conceivable that the Red Army could even give up its Far East temporarily and then strike back to take vengeance after settling scores elsewhere. In fact, neither China nor Japan would be willing to open a Far Eastern front in the face of certain failure to pin down the Soviet forces. No conventional army can hope to fight all the way across Siberia to Moscow, it would be nonsense to enter Siberia only to withdraw with the onset of winter.

C)   *The only possible and relatively inexpensive way for the Soviets to achieve their strategic objectives with low risk would be to push southward to the Indian Ocean.* Once established on the shores of the Indian Ocean, the Soviet Union could readily block vital oil supplies to Western countries, consolidate its alliances and friendships on the old Euro-Asian-African continent by extending its influence (eastward to India and Vietnam, westward to Libya and Algeria along the Mediterranean coast opposite Europe, southward to sweep across Africa), and finally *subdue Western Europe and Japan without waging costly and destructive wars there.*

However, the Red Army's southward thrust would go *not through the Near East to the Persian Gulf, but through Afghanistan-Baluchistan (A-B) to the Arabian Sea* to block the outlet of the Strait of Hormuz. The reasons are as follows:

1)   It would be difficult for the Soviets to fight across the Black Sea and the Caspian Sea; it would also be undesirable to wage war so near the rich Soviet Caucasus.

2)   The Near East is close to Europe and therefore accessible to American supplies and reinforcements.

3)   An invasion of Turkey is to be avoided because Turkey is a member of NATO and thus European NATO countries might become involved in the war.

4)   It would be undesirable for the USSR to get involved in any way in the Israeli-Islamic and Irani-Iraqi disputes. Moreover, currently pro-Soviet countries such as Iraq and Syria could become anti-Soviet if the Red Army were to reach the Persian Gulf by way of these countries. It would be wiser to let them concentrate their opposition against Israel—an American ally. Standing in the way, they might also impede the American access to the A-B region from the west.

5)   Compared with the Near East, the A-B region is economically backward and sociopolitically unstable. A war in such a region would stand to destroy little in the way of social wealth that the conqueror might wish to acquire. Moreover, the Soviet Union could play the role of emancipator by use of its 50 million Islamic population in the more developed Soviet Central Asia to "liberate" the A-B region from a feudal and tribal system. The Soviet Union could also exploit possible post-Khomeini turmoil in Iran and separatist upheavals such as the Paktunistan

Movement in Pakistan.

6)   The A-B region affords the Soviets their nearest corridor to warm water. Furthermore, the Red Army could make use of its superior conventional ground forces and its geographical advantage of maneuvering within a secure interior, while opposing American troops would suffer from a lack of assured and timely logistic supply and reinforcement.

In a nutshell, a major and decisive Soviet conventional offensive can succeed only in such a region: a geostrategic linchpin on the Soviet periphery, removed from easy American reach, in one of the poorest areas of the world. Neither NATO's southern and northern flanks nor the Near East would qualify. *The A-B region is the only one that qualifies on all counts.*

The invasion of Afghanistan in 1979 clearly revealed the Soviet strategic intention, although it was premature. In 1979 Brezhnev was prompted to take opportunistic advantage of the favorable external conditions (i.e., turmoil in Afghanistan and the American unpreparedness to react) to launch an invasion even though Soviet domestic conditions were not yet up to supporting his strategic ambition. We will certainly see the withdrawal of Soviet troops from Afghanistan in the near future. However, if the United States remains ill prepared, we will just as certainly see the Red Army coming back into Afghanistan some day within the next century after Gorbachev has accomplished his domestic *perestroika* and the Soviet leaders again deem it advisable to expand. The second invasion will doom the upcoming second detente as the first invasion killed the first detente.

A War Scenario in Baluchistan

Starting from Afghanistan, the mechanized Red Army could capture Baluchistan and reach the Arabian Sea in seven to ten days, and Soviet paratroopers could descend directly on the coast on the first day of the war. The difficulties for the United States in meeting the Soviet challenge in Baluchistan would be as follows:

A)   American military forces must react instantly because the war must be fought in the interior. If the Soviets reach the ocean, the Americans will lose the war. It is always difficult to fight a beachhead battle in a narrow coastal area with one's back to the ocean, and it would be impossible for the Americans to stage a large scale land operation from the vast Indian Ocean. To mount an immediate response, the United States must have prepositioned military storage in areas close to the battlefield, so that in case of emergency only personnel will need to be airlifted. Unfortunately, none of the countries around Baluchistan, *except China*, would be safe for U.S. military storage. The Islamic countries are unstable, and facilities there could be lost overnight, as happened in Iran. Israel could not provide safe storage bases either, not only because this would harm relationships between the United States and the Islamic countries and push them to the Soviet side, but also because the Soviets could invite their Islamic friends to strike American stockpiles in Israel. Furthermore, thanks to the nuclear asymmetry mentioned above, the Soviet Union could suppress Israel by nuclear blackmail.

B) In a conventional war between the two superpowers, given approximate parity in military technology and weaponry, neither would have a "super" power. The superior air force and fire power which the United States employed in Korea and Vietnam would be less effective in Baluchistan. There, what the United States should be prepared to fight is a large-scale and protracted land war involving probably more than one million American troops. Several naval task forces with a few Army and Marine divisions simply could not cope with the job. Unfortunately again, it would be very difficult for the United States to sustain such a war in Baluchistan for lack of safe lines of communication to ensure rapid delivery of reinforcements and logistic supplies to the area. Naval lines are slow and susceptible to interruption: modern technology (reconnaissance satellites, nuclear-powered propulsion systems, and guided weapons) favors the efficiency of attack submarines rather than surface ships. Moreover, thanks again to the above mentioned nuclear asymmetries, the Soviet Union could brandish its nuclear sword to deter Japan from hampering Soviet subs passing through the three strategic straits and to force the United States out of the sea-lanes altogether.

C) Airlift could be an alternative. It would not be practical, of course, to rely heavily on airlift operations from the U.S. mainland; military stockpiles and defense industries in Japan and Western Europe would have to be mobilized. However, most NATO stockpiles in Europe are encumbered by a potential threat from the Warsaw Pact, and the air routes from Europe to Baluchistan are not without impediments: Turkey has declared its opposition to stationing and passing of military material for use in areas outside NATO territory; Syria and Iraq probably would not let Americans pass unopposed through their airspace either; and the Soviet presence in

Libya, South Yemen, and Ethiopia must be considered. The routes from Japan and the Philippines to Baluchistan, *if not passing through China's mainland*, would have to be arranged far to the south to detour Vietnam and India.

China's Crucial Role

How might China contribute strategically to the preservation of world peace in the next century? Most strategists would say that China's crucial role is to tie up the Soviet forces in the Far East by threatening to open a second front. However, as we have already seen, such a threat seems unlikely to materialize as it would not succeed. Moreover, unless the Soviet Union were to initiate any attack on China, the Chinese would not necessarily consider themselves American allies nor would they be willing to get directly involved in hostilities between the superpowers. China's crucial role lies rather in the geostrategic advantages it can offer for the United States. Only by making full use of the advantages can the United States acquire *at the lowest cost* the most secure capability for rapid deployment, timely reinforcement, and sustained logistic supply to Baluchistan.

A)   To elaborate, it must be noted that China is not only a country of the Far East but also one of the two major countries in Central Asia (the other is the Soviet Union). The distance to Afghanistan's southern border from China's western border is 850 miles, about the same as the distance from Saudi Arabia and half of that from Israel or Egypt. The shortest routes from Japan and the Philippines to Baluchistan pass through China. China's other strong point is that the Soviet Union would not dare to punish China, either by nuclear attack or by conventional invasion, for its logistic support for American opposition to a southward Soviet expansion. The last thing the Soviet General Staff would want to initiate would be a major Soviet war with China. Such a war, by sapping Soviet strength that could otherwise be applied to the strategic priority of capturing the A-B region, would set the Soviet strategic master plan for global hegemony in total disarray.

B)   To support the United States in meeting the future Soviet challenge in the A-B region, China's geostrategic advantages could be of use in the following ways:

1)   Provision of the shortest and safest transportation routes

from Japan and the Philippines to the A-B region;

2)   Prestationing of military stockpiles in China's western territory within 2-3 hours' flight to the A-B region;

3)   Use of China's defense industry to produce military supplies for cheap and quick delivery to the A-B region, instead of transporting from the distant U.S. mainland;

4)   Safe provision in China's territorial air space for AWACS (Airborne Warning and Control Systems) to monitor Soviet war preparations in peacetime and to control air and ground operations in wartime.

C)   Such a strategic security cooperation could provide the most *cost-effective deterrence* against a Soviet southward offensive in the next century. Here are some of the ways in which American defense costs could be reduced:

1)   Airlift of military supplies to the A-B region from stockpiles in China and from bases in Japan and the Philippines (with air-refueling en route over China to allow for heavier cargo loads) could reduce U.S. spending on programs to develop new transport aircraft (e.g., C5B and C-17).

2)   Freed from heavy reliance on vulnerable sea-lanes, the United States could reduce its 600-warship program.

3)   Instead of wasting money to defend its straits and 1,000-mile surrounding sea area against Soviet naval incursion (an effort doomed to failure in the face of the Soviet nuclear bluff), Japan could play a more appropriate role by producing military material to be delivered through China to the A-B region.

4)   By utilizing the potential of China's defense industry, both the United States and Japan could reduce the costs of keeping domestic defense production lines running in peacetime, and of producing and transporting military supplies in wartime. China could also supply the necessities of life for American troops in the A-B region at much lower production and transportation costs. The same may be said for medical support.

5) Increased U.S. reliance on the East Asian line of communication through China to support a war in the A-B region would allow less strategic reliance on Israel, which would give the United States more room to maneuver in dealing with the Israeli-Islamic dispute and reduce the Soviet ability to exploit that dispute. It would also lighten the U.S. logistic reliance on European stockpiles, which would in turn allay many fears among NATO allies and make them more willing to detain Soviet forces in Europe during a war in the A-B region.

This concept of a PUJ security complementarity stems from an evaluation of the most likely region for Soviet expansion in the next century and can be summarized as follows:

The United States possesses strong armed forces to counter Soviet expansion in general but lacks a secured and efficient means to apply those forces to the particular battlefield where a Soviet military thrust is most likely to occur and where, when it occurs, it must be checked without delay.

Vast, populous, nuclear-independent and thus fearless China, though concerned with maintaining world peace, has neither the motive nor the military strength to engage in direct war against a Soviet expansion outside China's territory, but holds the uniquely advantageous geostrategic position to provide the fastest, safest, and least expensive logistic support for the United States in the area where the Soviet thrust is likely to occur.

Japan, nuclear-asymmetric and hence vulnerable to Soviet nuclear threat, is in a weak position to fight a direct war against the Soviet Union but possesses the high economic-industrial potential to provide strong logistic support in such a struggle; however, without China, Japan can serve as little better than a remote station in a broken supply line to the likely battlefield, and can contribute little to supporting the troops actually fighting to protect Japan's vital oil supply interest.

By combining the defense assets of the three countries, not only can we achieve the most effective and least expensive deterrence to the Soviet expansion in the next two or three decades but we may also prevent a major conventional war between the two superpowers with all the costs that would entail. The economic savings alone would greatly expedite world economic development, which in turn is the necessary material condition for a future peaceful convergence of the present bipolar world.

A COMPREHENSIVE ECONOMIC-SECURITY RELATIONSHIP

As we can see from this discussion, economic cooperation between China on the one hand and the United States and Japan on the other cannot go far and fast without a concomitant strategic cooperation. As long as China's valuable strategic potential remains unused, it will not have the capital to enter into large-scale economic exchange. At the same time, the Western countries are exhausted with spending to maintain their precarious security while their domestic markets are insufficient to bring their economic potential into full play. Economic complementarity and security complementarity between nations are usually seen as two discrete concerns. In the case of the United States, Japan, and China, however, as long as the two complementarities are treated separately, none of the three can extract much benefit. Only by combining complementarities through a well designed, comprehensive economic-security program can peace be achieved at a manageable cost, as well as the accelerated economic growth for all the countries concerned.

It may be enlightening to remember what Deng Xiaoping said in October 1984: "Many problems may not be solved by going along the old way. Can we find a new way? New problems can only be solved by going a new way. Our brain must think out some new ideas if we want to stabilize the world." Before the concept of a comprehensive PUJ economic-security relationship can be seen as acceptable by incumbent and future leaders of all three countries, some wrong or obsolete perceptions and policies must be corrected.

The Taiwan Issue

It is worthwhile to mention Deng Xiaoping's criticism that, "Americans have been short-sighted; they can see only small things but not big problems." The U.S. government must recognize that China's reunification is not detrimental to, but compatible with, American interest.

A)   The PRC stands out as a regional power of global significance in light of the fact that, with respect to security planning, the A-B region is the American Achilles heel and the United States cannot protect its interest there without China's logistic assistance. However, it will be impossible for China to effectuate this assistance as long as the United States pursues a policy of negative interference in China's reunification. Indeed, to make strategic cooperation feasible, it will not be enough for the American government simply to stop its negative interference. It should take some *positive* action to expedite China's reunification, not only because the United States needs China's help but also because the United States is obligated to right the historic wrong which has kept the Taiwan issue so far unresolved.

B)   Taiwan has lost most of its former value in the American strategic equation unless the United States expects to resume a U.S.-China confrontation, which in the present global context is strategically unsound. It is also logically absurd: the Taiwan issue itself, if unresolved, is the one issue most likely to cause future confrontation between the United States and China, yet the possibility of such a confrontation is commonly cited as a major justification for continued U.S. obstruction of a resolution. A far more reasonable policy would recognize that Taiwan can become strategically important to the United States again, but *only* when the island, as a part of reunified China, serves as a link in a logistic supply line stretching across China's mainland to the A-B region.

C)   Mainly as a result of its unbalanced trade with the United States, Taiwan has accumulated more than $75 billion in foreign reserves. Today its per capita foreign reserve is the highest in the world and still growing. In an attempt to reverse this trend, the United States has been imposing some protectionist measures that have hurt both the U.S. and the Taiwanese economies. An optimal solution to the problem would be for Taiwan to invest its surplus dollars in economic construction on the mainland through importation of American equipment and technology. This importation could be further expanded if the mainland were to supply Taiwan with raw materials and other products to reduce Taiwan's hard currency spending to procure these items abroad.

Japan's Role

The question of how much Japan should spend on defense has long been a matter for debate, especially since Japan's emergence as an economic superpower. Critics in the United States complain that Japan has enjoyed a free ride for too long and urge, so far not quite successfully, that Japan share more of the burden of defending its own interests. The other Asian-Pacific countries, recalling the grave days of World War II, worry about a possible revival of Japanese militarism and are angered by American initiatives to encourage Japanese rearmament. Inside Japan, the 1 percent of GNP criterion has become a watershed: those who favor a higher percentage spent for defense are seen as hawkish militarists, those who favor less than 1 percent, dovish pacifists. All this debate misses the point. First of all, as the above strategic analysis indicates, as long as Japan remains nuclear-asymmetric it cannot play any military role outside its homeland in direct confrontation with the Soviet Union, no matter how much it may spend on defense. Second, Japan cannot today repeat its militaristic achievements of the early 1940s: sweeping through all Indochina to the Burma-India border, controlling Singapore and most of Indonesia down to Rabaul and Bougainville in Melanesia, occupying the Philippines and assaulting Micronesia. Nor can Japan move again to conquer the Korean Peninsula and Taiwan on the grounds that they are two pillars necessary to Japan's expansion. All that is history, past and gone. The international geopolitical and economic-technological environment has changed totally since World War II. In this nuclear world, Japan, a small but densely populated island country short on natural resources and set in an ocean girded by major powers, can never become a principal military power again no matter how much it spends on weaponry and not even if it were to develop a nuclear arsenal. All internal and external conditions suggest that the talented Japanese people should remain primarily economy-oriented. Therefore, it is not out of concern about the revival of Japanese militarism but rather out of a goodwill wish not to see Japan waste money that we oppose an increased Japanese military expenditure. To avoid being a free rider, Japan ought instead to act as a military logistic producer and supplier in wartime and to assist China economically in peacetime, all by way of payment for the American use of China's geostrategic position to protect Japanese oil supplies. In addition, it should be mentioned that, to a certain extent, Japan owes its present economic prosperity to China's generosity in not claiming war reparations.

Nonalignment and Interdependence

The PRC is a Third World country and it will not alter its existing policy of nonalignment to either superpower. However, this is not to say that China is intent upon implementing a policy of precise equidistance. In fact, in this strategically bipolar world, none of the third world countries can maintain a clearly equidistant posture vis-à-vis the two superpowers because no absolutely neutral center-line exists between the two poles. Short of direct military alliance, a comprehensive economic-security relationship with either superpower does not suffice to negate a Third World country's nonaligned status. Egypt and Pakistan, Cuba and Ethiopia afford examples on either side. The American use of Egypt's Ras Banas airbase on the Red Sea coast and the annual joint military exercises in which thousands of

American troops are airlifted from the U.S. mainland to Egypt have not made Egypt an all-out ally of the United States. How could some joint military stockpiles in China and overflight rights for logistic supplies in case of emergency, without direct Chinese involvement in war actions, be interpreted as a military alliance with a superpower? In fact, China provided logistic supply lines for the Soviet Union during the war in Vietnam even while China's leaders were routinely condemning Soviet social imperialism and Chinese troops were defending against Soviet aggression on the Ussuri River. This shows that it is not impossible and inconsistent for a Third World nation to help one superpower to deter another superpower which it deems more expansionist and more dangerous to global security at a particular time and in a particular place. Supporting one superpower in a region where it is defensively opposing the other superpower's expansionism does not bar China from criticizing and even acting against the former superpower's imperialist behavior in other regions.

For Third World countries only recently freed from imperialist oppression, national independence is a particularly precious asset. They must be very cautious about entering into comprehensive economic-security relationships with developed countries with past or present imperialist records. Nonetheless, there can be no absolute independence in today's interdependent world. While less powerful allies and friends depend upon a superpower's protection, the superpower is reciprocally dependent on support from its allies and friends to protect its status vis-à-vis another superpower. Similarly, debtor and creditor countries are interdependent, and that is why today's international debt crisis worries them all. The degrees of dependence of one upon another are often unequal in certain areas, to be sure. However, it is foolish to go isolationist for fear of becoming more dependent. If you feel more dependent in one area, it would be wiser to find another interdependent or complementary area where your counterpart is more dependent upon you, so that a roughly balanced interdependence in general would satisfy all parties concerned.

The Sino-U.S. interdependence is memorably acknowledged in Henry Kissinger's memoirs, where he writes:

... Mao could be brutal in cutting to the heart of a problem. On one of my later trips I commented to Deng Xiaoping that the relations of our two countries were on a sound basis because neither asked anything of the other. The next day Mao referred to my comment. . . He firmly rebutted my banality: "If neither side had anything to ask from the other, why would you be coming to Peking? If neither side had anything to ask, then why would we want to receive you and the President?"

The PUJ economic-security relationship will be of an interdependent nature, with many things to be asked of each country by the others. In weighing economic cooperation alone, we have to admit that although it will be mutually beneficial, China will be the most dependent party because China would be most severely hurt if a large-scale, long-term economic cooperation program were to begin and then be suspended suddenly for whatever reason. However, the Western countries would be more dependent as far as the security component is concerned. An abrupt Chinese withdrawal from the security cooperation would upset all major defense arrangements, with potentially catastrophic consequences. As a total package, though, the integrated economic-security relationship would effect a well balanced interdependence.

Nevertheless, unless the ruling bodies of *all three* countries conclude it is necessary to inject new thinking into their foreign policies, and unless they also become convinced that the arguments given in this chapter are both sound and practicable, a comprehensive PRC-USA-Japan economic-security relationship will remain an unreachable goal, a matter of purely academic interest, and we will to let this mutually beneficial economic opportunity slip by. Worse than that and in the worst case, peace may well come to an end in the next century when the Soviet Union, after a successful *perestroika*, deems it favorable to end the second detente.

NOTES

[1]The term "traditional" here refers to the *functions* which the infrastructural, or second-wave, industries perform, not to the technologies on which they are based.

7

U.S. Military Relationships in East Asia and the Pacific: A Long View
Edward B. Baker

Undoubtedly, a sound appreciation of the importance of the Pacific Basin to the security of the United States is essential to the planning and execution of defense relationships in that region. Unfortunately, during periods of severe budgetary belt-tightening, it becomes obvious that many people, including some in Washington, harbor misconceptions about what we do in East Asia, why we do it, and how it affects our national interest. These misconceptions, if not corrected, could undermine the foundation of the most successful regional policy the United States has at work in the world today.

To understand U.S. security considerations in the Pacific Basin in the 1990s requires, in the first instance, an appreciation of our overall defense strategy. That strategy is and has been to deter aggression. It depends on clear alliance commitments and ready forces capable of an effective and credible response to any level of aggression. Equally important is our adversaries' perception of our capabilities and our commitments. The defense policies that support our strategy of deterrence are designed to ensure that potential adversaries do not underestimate our commitment to our own vital interests and those of our allies. This is the crux of the problem we face currently, and it is the challenge we face in the decade ahead. The defense policies referred to are: an advantageous *balance of forces*; provision for *forward deployed forces*; an effective and credible system of *alliances*; and the *flexibility* to respond to any and all contingencies.

BALANCE OF FORCES

The determination of what constitutes an advantageous balance of forces in any region is not an easy task. Simply put, the United States and its allies must maintain military capabilities sufficient to deter aggression. A key variable in that equation is, of course, an understanding and appreciation of the current and future threat.

Approximately one-third of the Soviet Union's total forces were deployed in the Soviet Far East and the Pacific in 1988: approximately 55 Soviet divisions, with personnel numbering between 11,000 and 13,500 each, were deployed along the Sino-Soviet border; the Soviet Pacific fleet is still the largest of the Soviet navy's four fleets, with more than 80 surface combatants, 90 attack submarines, and 500 naval aircraft; the Soviet Pacific air force has more than 350 long range bombers and 2,000 tactical aircraft. And the Soviet military forces are modernizing and developing their capability to project military power beyond their borders.

With this present-day military muscle behind him, General Secretary Mikhail Gorbachev has made it clear, in speeches at Vladivostok on 28 July 1986 and at Krasnoyarsk on 16 September 1988, that the Soviet Union intends to expand its role in East Asian and Pacific affairs. Gorbachev's statements reflect his concern about Soviet exclusion from the dynamic development of the Pacific Basin and about the state of Soviet political and economic influence in the region.

Soviet strategy in East Asia and the Pacific now focuses on limiting U.S. influence and weakening our alliances in the region, containing and isolating China from the United States and Japan, and cultivating relations with the ASEAN nations and the island states of the South Pacific. In Northeast Asia, the Soviets seek primarily to reduce what they perceive as a growing U.S.-Japan-PRC barrier to Soviet interests. In Southeast Asia and the Pacific, their major aim is to undermine the U.S. presence and establish their own foothold. To date, the familiar Soviet approach has been to build up disproportionate military power, dramatize fears of nuclear war, and offer solutions to the alleged war danger in the form of confidence-building measures, nuclear free zones, and multilateral and bilateral consultations with the USSR.

The big question is whether the Soviets will continue these efforts through the 1990s. For the near term—actions speak louder than words, and it remains to be seen what Gorbachev will actually do to promote renewed Soviet interest in East Asia and the Pacific—it is predictable that the Soviets will have a difficult time establishing their relevance to the major concerns of the nations of the region. Consequently, the United States can expect them to place continued emphasis on what they do well: build and field military forces with a force projection punch.

It is important to note also that the size of the Soviets' military presence and the pattern of their deployment in the 1990s will be affected by the state of Sino-Soviet relations, the retention of Soviet access to Cam Ranh Bay in Vietnam, the success of Soviet efforts to penetrate the South Pacific, and perhaps most importantly, their perception of the U.S. military capability in the region.

The last point raises a critical question: will the United States and its regional friends and allies be able to maintain their strength in the face of the Soviet challenge? One should turn first to Japan for part of the answer. Japan's defense effort has already become meaningful in the 1980s (Japan's defense outlay is now sixth largest in the world and second among non-nuclear powers). This effort will become increasingly important in the 1990s (when Japan will likely surpass the United Kingdom and France to become fourth in the world lineup), but only as a complement to U.S. forces in the Western Pacific. Let there be no question, U.S. forces provide the real basis for Japanese security.

The defense roles Japan has chosen, a high-technology   air, anti-submarine, and anti-invasion defense of its territory, air, and sea-lanes to 1000 miles, seriously impact on Soviet Pacific planning because Japan lies immediately due east of the key Soviet naval port of Vladivostok. Japan can effectively deny Soviet ships and aircraft undetected access to the Pacific and even the Indian Ocean when those forces come from the Vladivostok area.

In the 1990s, the Japanese air defense and anti-submarine forces will increase their capability from the minimum necessary for self-defense to an enhanced capability by adding broad area surveillance systems, such as Over the Horizon Radar (OTHR) and AWACS, refuelable aircraft systems to make their already numerous first-rate fighter interceptors more capable, and sophisticated land- and sea-based air defense platforms (Patriot and Aegis, if the U.S. Congress allows). These systems will make undetected Soviet shipping or aircraft access to the Pacific or to Japanese territory through the Sea of Japan severely complicated. Thus, Japan's enhanced defense capability, complemented by U.S. strategic and conventional capabilities, presents a very favorable scenario for continued deterrence in the Northwest Pacific.

Korea is the next consideration. The armed forces of the Republic of Korea (ROK) have increased their capability significantly during the 1980s. The ROK has pursued a well planned, sustained Force Improvement Program which has narrowed the gap between North and South. The 1990s will probably see the emergence of a true military balance on the Korean Peninsula, with ROK forces roughly comparable to North Korean forces, while the economy of the South continues to rocket ahead of the stagnating North. What remains uncertain is the role of the United States in Korea. A number of factors, including the forward deployment of a large North Korean force along the Demilitarized Zone (DMZ), the proximity of Seoul to that zone, the likely disparity in economic wealth between North and South, and the established pattern of irrational behavior on the part of the communist leaders in North Korea, would appear to make the presence of U.S. forces on or near the Korean Peninsula an important requirement for South Korean security in the next decade. Obviously, U.S. forces will remain in South Korea only as long as the ROK government desires; however, no one should doubt that the functions the United States serves in Korea today--as role model, friend, and partner--are necessary and successful ones. Loose talk about a unilateral abrogation of the U.S. defense commitment in Korea is irresponsible and potentially harmful, and it does not represent the view of the U.S. Government.

Another key player in the region is China. Predicting the military situation within the political dynamics of China is a precarious undertaking even for those who have dedicated considerable time and effort to the study of the Middle Kingdom.

What about Southeast Asia? The armed forces of U.S. friends and allies in Southeast Asia will remain modest in size and technological sophistication in the 1990s, and exclusively defensive in capability. The pace of military modernization will be slow, with the nations of the region focusing their primary energies on economic and social development. Will Vietnamese forces continue to occupy Cambodia? It seems certain that even at the conclusion of their troops' withdrawal, the Vietnamese will pursue their long standing goal of dominating Indochina. Political instability will undoubtedly characterize some of the developing nations in the region. In the 1990s these countries, anxious to preserve their independence and fearful of the "coercive diplomacy" practiced by the Soviets and their Vietnamese ally, will continue to see their security bound up in a strong U.S. military presence at Philippine air and naval bases and at sea in the Western Pacific.

As for Down Under, the coming decade will see the Australian Defense Forces continuing as a highly trained, well equipped professional military force. In its recently published White Paper on Defense, the Australian Government presented a blueprint for the future in terms of national strategy, force structure, and modernization. By fulfilling the requirements of that White Paper in the 1990s, Australia will make a significant contribution to regional security and reconfirm Australia's commitment to the Western Alliance.

It seems clear that the single most important determinant of U.S. military relationships in East Asia and the Pacific in the 1990s will not be political conditions inside the nations of the region or their rate of economic growth, although these will be important factors. Rather, America's ability to enjoy continued access to the peoples, resources, and markets of Asia and to keep the confidence of friends and allies in the region will rest in large measure on the ability of the United States to maintain, with its allies, that military superiority which ensures and protects a continuing complementarity of interests.

FORWARD DEPLOYED FORCES

The maintenance of U.S. military superiority in East Asia and the Pacific depends on its forward deployed forces. Because the United States cannot adequately defend its interests with U.S.-based forces alone, it now maintains ground and air forces in Japan, the Republic of Korea, and the Philippines, and naval carrier battle groups and marine amphibious forces in the Western Pacific. These forward deployed forces are visible manifestations of American power and of the American resolve to meet its security commitments.

Forward deployed U.S. forces depend on two vital conditions in order to perform their missions successfully: the support of the American people, acting through their elected representatives in Congress to give the U.S. military the wherewithal to fight; and the willingness of U.S. allies and friends in the region to grant basing rights, port visits, and overflight privileges.

A STRONG SYSTEM OF ALLIANCES

Alliances are an important element in U.S. defense policy formation for East Asia. Five of the eight U.S. mutual security treaties presently in force are treaties with East Asian nations: Japan, Korea, Thailand, the Philippines, and Australia. These alliances enable a sharing of common security burdens and a division of labor designed to capitalize on the relative strengths of each nation. U.S. alliances have made it possible for all member nations to achieve a level of deterrence and defense that otherwise would be unattainable for any one of them alone or without U.S. participation. Furthermore, regional cooperation in defense matters reinforces political cohesion and improves diplomatic and economic relationships.

At present, the health of these security alliances in East Asia and the Pacific is generally sound, but what is the prognosis for the 1990s?

With Japan, the issue will be burden sharing. Barring a change in roles, the Japanese will be able to finance their defense efforts in the 1990s for something less than 1.5 percent of GNP and perhaps for as little as 1.1 or 1.2 percent. If the Japanese were to spend as much as 3 percent of GNP on defense, as some U.S. congressmen have urged, Japan would quickly be transformed into a military superpower spending in excess of $100 billion annually and easily able to finance a strategic nuclear and offensive arsenal. Neither the Japanese people nor their Asian neighbors support this role for Japan. However, as other contributors to this volume have demonstrated, there is much Japan can do to increase its share of the alliance responsibility without the politically destabilizing effects of a huge increase in defense spending. The developing U.S.-Japan defense relationship is a dynamic, symbiotic, up-to-date cooperative effort that contributes greatly to the continued security of both countries and the region.

The U.S. security arrangement with the Republic of Korea in the 1990s will be strong, but its character will be altered by the maturing of the Korean political system and the increasing sophistication of its military forces. The 1990s may see a continued need for the presence of U.S. forces in or near the ROK, but most likely the system that ties ROK and U.S. forces together under an American commander will be changed. At the same time, South Korea's economic success will describe for it a larger role in offsetting the costs of U.S. forces there.

The U.S. security relationships with Thailand and the Philippines will remain intact in the 1990s. Not only are these alliances important for the two countries involved, but also they serve as a key element in regional security in Southeast Asia. There is a strong possibility that the United States and the Philippine government will reach a mutually acceptable agreement to extend American military presence at Clark Air Force Base and Subic Bay.

The regional stability created by the ANZUS Treaty now rests solely on the close security cooperation existing between Australia and the United States. The suspension of the U.S. security obligation to New Zealand illustrates just how serious Washington is about military relationships contributing to the U.S. defense strategy of deterrence. Australian-U.S. cooperation, like the alliance on which it is founded, will remain a cornerstone of U.S. defense policy in the 1990s.

FLEXIBILITY

To a marked extent, U.S. forward deployments and contingency plans for U.S. forces in the region reflect the best judgment of the U.S. military planners about the source and seriousness of likely aggression. No one can be certain, however, about the time, location, or nature of future aggressive actions. Therefore, American capabilities, plans, and ways of thinking must be flexible enough to enable effective responses to unexpected contingencies.

The need for flexibility increases the importance of strategic mobility—that is, the ability of the United States to deploy and sustain forces over great distances. In the vast maritime region of the Pacific, this factor has special salience. With the expansion of Soviet capabilities for projecting power, flexibility will be a critical element in U.S. defense policy in the 1990s.

And, flexibility has other dimensions. As the nations of the region grow and develop, we will be faced more frequently with ideas and proposals that do not appear immediately attractive. The U.S. response to these schemes must be measured and thoughtful. For example, if nuclear-tree zones are not advantageous to U.S. defense policy, we must nevertheless recognize that they reflect a bona fide fear of nuclear weapons present among many friendly nations. Americans need to be flexible as listeners so that they can make their own case convincingly. Flexibility does not demand a vacillating policy, but it does require that the United States listen carefully to its friends and allies, and to its adversaries as well. That, after all, is intrinsic to the leadership role. Moreover, a strong America that invests wisely in effective deterrence and maintains military superiority need not fear coping with the dynamics of political, economic, and social change that will certainly emerge in East Asia and the Pacific in the 1990s.

8

United States-Chinese Military Relations: Implications for Japan
Edward W. Ross

The development of U.S.-PRC military relations began soon after the normalization of diplomatic relations between the United States and the People's Republic of China on January 1, 1979. Like the establishment of diplomatic relations itself, the development of the military relationship was a result of a willingness on both sides to pursue policies aimed at satisfing each country's basic interests for both the near and the long term. Neither Beijing nor Washington today seeks strategic partnership, and numerous differences exist, and will continue to exist, with respect to the two countries' approaches to domestic and foreign policy. Nevertheless, the several important issues on which the two countries agree provide ample incentive for both sides to engage in military interaction and technological cooperation.

As Winston Lord, U.S. Ambassador to China, pointed out in 1986, "We share numerous security concerns with the Chinese:

- We agree that Vietnam should get out of Cambodia;
- We agree that the Soviet Union should get out of Afghanistan;
- We agree that there must be global limits on intermediate range nuclear missiles in Europe and Asia;
- We agree that conflict on the Korean Peninsula would be a disaster and therefore we should seek ways to reduce tensions and maintain peace;
- We agree that good relations with Japan are beneficial all around; and,
- We agree, quietly, that a substantial U.S. presence in Asia serves the cause of regional peace."[1]

The development of U.S.-Chinese military relations, therefore, reflects the growing importance of China as a positive element of U.S. foreign policy in Asia, as a complement to the strategic relationship between the United States and Japan, and as a potentially significant contributor to the peace and stability of Asia and the world. Although the expansion of Chinese military capability that is likely to result from this relationship presents some risk for the United States and its friends and allies in the region, the potential benefits appear to outweigh the risks. The United States seeks an enduring military relationship with China in the belief that a more secure, modernizing, and friendly China, a China with an independent foreign policy but an economic system compatible with the West, can make a significant contribution to peace, stability, and economic prosperity throughout the region. To further this end, the United States sought to play a positive role in China's military modernization—a role that not only served the mutual interests of the United States and China, but also took into account the concerns and interests of U.S. friends and allies in the region.[2]

Beijing's motivation for closer military relations with the United States sprang from a desire to obtain the technology needed for a military modernization consistent with its own long-term strategic goals of establishing China as a world power. Certainly the tragic events of June 1989 at Beijing's Tiananmen Square has influenced the relatively smooth U.S.-Chinese cooperation. Nevertheless it is also clear that it would serve neither U.S. nor Chinese interests to demolish a useful relationship built up so carefully over two decades.

All these considerations have important implications for China's neighbors, who watch with great interest as China's industrial, agricultural, scientific and technological, and military modernization unfolds. Japan in particular watches with mixed emotions. On one hand, Japan welcomes the opportunities for new markets and investments intrinsic in Chinese modernization. On the other hand, Japan does not wish to see a militarily powerful China emerge to threaten or dominate the region.

This paper examines the development of U.S.-China military relations and ponders the implications for Japan. It first reviews significant developments to date in U.S.-China military relations, then assesses prospects for future development and the likely impact of the relationship on Chinese military capabilities, and finally, discusses the Japanese perspective.

1979-1983: THE FIRST STEPS

Secretary of Defense Harold Brown's visit to Beijing in January 1980, followed by then Deputy Chief of the General Staff Liu Huaqing's visit to the United States in May 1980 and soon-to-be Minister of Defense Geng Biao's visit to the United States a month later, provided the initial steps toward a dialogue between the military establishments of the two countries. The beginning of a new U.S. policy with regard to the Chinese military was reflected in the announcement by Secretary of State Alexander Haig in June 1981 that the United States was ready to consider the sale, on a case-by-case basis, of defensive weapons and equipment to the People's Republic of China.

The further development of the relationship was hampered somewhat in 1981 and 1982 by several factors. Important among these were an internal Chinese policy debate over the extent to which the PRC ought to seek foreign participation in its defense modernization, and continuing differences between the United States and China over the future status of Taiwan. In August 1982, however, the United States and China signed a joint communiqué concerning U.S. arms sales to Taiwan, and by the latter half of 1983 a growing consensus within China favored further development of U.S.-China military relations.[3]

Two important U.S. visits to China in 1983 also contributed to the advancement of the military relationship. The first was the visit in August by Secretary of Commerce Malcolm Baldridge, which led to a liberalization of U.S. guidelines for the sale of seven categories of dual-use items to the PRC. The second was the visit of Secretary of Defense Caspar Weinberger in September. These two exchanges occurred at a time of significant growth in political and economic relations between the United States and China. Moreover, they signaled an acknowledgement by both sides that the expansion of military contacts was a natural by-product of normal relations between friendly, non-allied countries.

Weinberger's visit was particularly significant in that it established the framework for expansion of U.S.-Chinese military contacts. The secretary's visit resumed and extended the high-level dialogue between senior U.S. and Chinese military leaders begun by Secretary Brown in 1980. It laid the groundwork for subsequent functional military exchanges between the services of the two country's armed forces. Finally, it identified and articulated to the Chinese military leadership several military mission areas, keyed to Chinese requests, that could benefit from future military technology cooperation between the two countries. In addition, it energized a U.S. interagency review process designed to ensure a consistent U.S. policy with respect to military technology cooperation.[4]

THE THREE PILLARS

From September 1983 on, U.S.-China military relations would rest on three pillars of mutual support: high-level visits, functional military exchanges, and technology cooperation.

High-level visits are those reciprocal exchange visits by the most senior U.S. and Chinese military and defense leaders. Individuals who fall into this category number no more than a dozen or so on both sides. They are the defense ministers, the chairman of the joint chiefs/chief of the general staff, the service chiefs (and service secretaries on the U.S. side), the U.S. Commander-in-Chief Pacific, and certain deputy chiefs of the Chinese general staff. The primary objectives of reciprocal high-level visits on both sides is to foster an exchange of views on regional and global security issues and to educate the senior military leaders on each side about the military establishment of the other.

Functional military exchanges encompass the entire spectrum of military-to-military interactions below the highest level, exclusive of those visits and exchanges dealing with specific military technology cooperation programs. Primarily, functional military exchanges consist of visits by commanders and members of one country's military units and functional organizations to counterpart units and organizations in the other country. They also include such things as ship visits and visits by various demonstration teams and entertainment groups. These exchanges enable greater numbers of military personnel to learn about the other country and to exchange information in their functional specialties. This kind of interaction adds depth to the international relationship and improves the likelihood that future U.S. and Chinese military leaders will share some common frame of reference.

Military technology cooperation refers to the transfer of military equipment and technology through foreign military sales (FMS) and commercial channels. U.S. military sales to China fall into two general categories: dual-use equipment and technology, licensed by the Department of Commerce; and end items and technologies controlled by the international munitions list (IML) and licensed by the Department of State. Of primary significance for the military relationship are weapons, equipment, and technologies associated with the IML.

HIGH-LEVEL VISITS

From 1983 on, numerous high-level visits by officials of both countries have served to maintain momentum in the developing relationship and to provide direction for functional exchanges and military technology cooperation.

One such visit was that of Chinese Defense Minister Zhang Aiping, who journeyed to the United States in June 1984 in reciprocation of Secretary Weinberger's September 1983 visit to China. In addition to meeting with Weinberger, Zhang had discussions with President Ronald Reagan and Secretary of State George Shultz, and with Chairman of the Joint Chiefs of Staff General John Vessey and other senior military officials. This initial exchange of visits between the two defense leaders laid the foundation for a pattern of reciprocal visits between senior defense officials and military leaders. Each visit further advanced the bilateral military relationship.

A visit to China in August 1984 by Secretary of the Navy John Lehman, as the guest of People's Liberation Army (PLA) Navy Commander Liu Huaqing, opened the door to direct navy-to-navy contacts. Secretary Lehman's visit also established a dialogue that eventually led to the PASSEX (passing exercise) conducted between the two navies in January 1986 in the South China Sea. Although such courtesy exercises are conducted routinely between the U.S. Navy and the navies of numerous friendly and allied nations, China's participation must be seen as a. noteworthy step in the military relationship.

General Vessey and Admiral William J. Crowe, U.S. Commander-in-Chief Pacific (CINCPAC), visited China in January 1985 as guests of Chief of the General Staff Yang Dezhi. Standing for several hours in sub-zero weather during a visit to a PLA training area in Shenyang, Vessey and Crowe became the first U.S. military leaders to observe a PLA "combined service" training exercise. Like Weinberger, Vessey pursued discussions of regional and global issues with his Chinese hosts.

Chief of Staff of the Air Force General Charles Gabriel visited China in October 1985 as the guest of PLA Air Force Commander Wang Hai. The two air force leaders agreed to exchanges of training and logistics delegations and discussed ways to further the air force-to-air force relationship, and, in the process established a close personal rapport. (In their discussion of Korean War experiences, it came to light that Wang, a Chinese ace during the war, may have been shot down by Gabriel.)

PLA Navy Commander Liu Huaqing visited the United States in November as the guest of the Chief of Naval Operations Admiral James Watkins. Liu met with Secretary Lehman and other Navy and Defense leaders in Washington and thereafter toured U.S. Navy installations in Florida, San Diego, and Hawaii. Admiral Watkins visited China in April 1986 as Liu's guest.[5] The two navy leaders continued their discussions on ways to expand navy-to-navy interaction.

In May 1986, Yang Dezhi, Chief of the PLA general staff, made his reciprocal visit to the United States and was the guest of Admiral Crowe, General Vessey's successor as Chairman of the Joint Chiefs of Staff. Yang met with Secretary Weinberger and Assistant Secretary of Defense Richard Armitage and, like his colleagues before him, visited U.S. military installations on the continent and in Hawaii.

Secretary Weinberger returned to China in early October 1986, almost exactly three years after his initial visit to China. The visit came at a time when significant progress toward reaching agreement on a major cooperative FMS program had been made, and resulted in the announcement of a U.S. Navy ship visit to China in November. In addition, Weinberger engaged his host, Defense Minister Zhang Aiping, and other Chinese political and military leaders in a dialogue on numerous regional and global issues ranging from China's conflict with Vietnam to U.S.-Soviet arms control discussions. Chinese leaders who received Weinberger included Deng Xiaoping, Premier Zhao Ziyang, Secretary General of the Military Commission Yang Shangkun, Yang Dezhi, and Foreign Minister Wu Xueqian. Zhang welcomed Weinberger as an "old friend" with the special gesture of a small private dinner on the evening of his arrival and stressed the personal goodwill between himself and Secretary Weinberger on several occasions during the visit.

While the U.S. defense secretary was in Beijing, another senior Chinese military leader, Hong Xuezhi, director of the General Logistics Department of the PLA, led a group of Chinese logisticians on a visit to the United States as guests of Dr. James Wade, Assistant Secretary of Defense for Acquisition and Logistics. Hong departed Beijing on the evening of Weinberger's arrival. The two met briefly in the Great Hall of the People along with Yang Shangkun and Yang Dezhi.

Since Weinberger's second visit to China, the exchange of high-level visits between senior U.S. and Chinese military leaders has continued apace. U.S. Army Chief of Staff General John Wickham visited China in late November 1986 as the guest of PLA Deputy Chief of the General Staff Xu Xin. Marine Corps Commandant Paul X. Kelley visited China in March 1987 and PLA Air Force Commander Wang Hai visited the United States in April. Military Commission Vice Chairman Yang Shangkun, the most senior Chinese military leader next to Deng Xiaoping himself, visited the United States in May as head of a Chinese delegation. Yang, the guest of then Vice President George Bush, met with President Reagan, Secretary of State Shultz, Secretary Weinberger, and leaders of both the House and Senate. In June, Admiral Ronald Hays, Commander-in-Chief Pacific, visited China as the guest of Deputy Chief of the General Staff Xu Xin. In September 1987 Secretary of the Air Force Edward Aldridge visited China and led the first U.S. defense delegation on a visit to Tibet.

As of this writing, the most recent high-level visit in the ongoing series was the visit to China in September 1988 of Secretary of Defense Frank Carlucci. Secretary Carlucci was the guest of Defense Minister Qin Jiwei.

In each case, visits by senior U.S. and Chinese military leaders have expanded communications and understanding between the two armed forces and paved the way for increased contacts. Thus the pattern of high-level exchange visits begun by Secretary Weinberger and Minister Zhang Aiping in 1983-1984 has set the overall tone for the military relationship between the two countries and provided a framework for functional exchanges between the various military organizations and for cooperative technology programs.

FUNCTIONAL MILITARY EXCHANGES

Although reciprocal training and logistics exchanges took place in late 1980 and early 1981, the current pattern for such exchanges resulted from discussions held during Secretary Weinberger's September 1983 visit to China. At that time General William Richardson, representing the Joint Chiefs of Staff, as deputy commander of the U.S. Army Training and Doctrine Command (TRADOC), met with Zhang Tong, director of the Foreign Affairs Bureau (FAB) of the Ministry of Defense. The purpose of their meeting was to discuss functional military exchanges to be conducted in 1984, and during the meeting the two sides agreed to a new round of training and logistics exchanges. Subsequently, a PLA training delegation visited the United States in April 1984 and a PLA logistics delegation visited in May. Reciprocal U.S. training and logistics delegations traveled to China in October and November 1984 respectively. Each of these delegations contained tri-service representation.

As the bilateral relationship matured throughout 1984 and 1985, functional service-to-service contacts diversified. The U.S. Army TRADOC hosted a training seminar in August 1985. In January 1986 the first operational contact between U.S. and Chinese forces took place in the South China Sea, where elements of the U.S. Seventh Fleet conducted a PASSEX and met and exchanged greetings at sea with ships of the PLA Navy. Although the PASSEX was terminated early owing to heavy seas and turbulent weather, it was a significant milestone in the military relationship.

In September 1986 the PLA Air Force Song and Dance Troupe visited the United States. Beginning its tour in Washington, D.C., with a performance in the National Theater, the troupe then visited various military installations and performed at each stop for the U.S. forces stationed there and for the general public. A reciprocal visit to China by the U.S. Air Force Band took place in June 1987.

By the end of 1986, progress in the military relationship was reflected by an increased scope and frequency of functional interaction. On November 5, 1986, three ships of the U.S. Seventh Fleet, the U.S.S. *Reeves*, a guided missile cruiser, the destroyer U.S.S. *Oldendorf*, and the U.S.S. *Rentz*, a guided missile frigate, began a seven-day port call to the Chinese city of Qingdao. Admiral James A. Lyons, Commander-in-Chief, Pacific Fleet, was the senior U.S. Naval officer involved. This historic ship visit to China gave U.S. and Chinese forces their first large-scale opportunity to interact face to face.[6] Just ten days following the ship visit, the first PLA navy logistics delegation arrived in the United States, and on December 1 a Department of Defense (DOD) quality assurance delegation arrived in China. December also saw visits to the United States by a PLA medical delegation and the first PLA air force maintenance delegation.

Functional military visits in 1987 included visits to China by a joint U.S. mid-level management team in January, the commander of U.S. Air Force logistics in February, a joint U.S. systems analysis team led by Deputy Under Secretary of the Army Walter Hollis in March, and a U.S. Navy training delegation led by Vice Admiral Maxwell Thunman in April. In September, during Air Force Secretary Aldridge's visit to China, the U.S. Air Force Thunderbirds demonstration team performed at Beijing for a crowd of over 5,000 PLA personnel, including senior officers from all over China. The third annual PLA/U.S. Army training seminar took place in October. In November, a U.S. Air Force maintenance delegation visited China, and a joint U.S.-China National Defense University conference was held in China. Finally, a PLA Air Force aircraft preservation team visited the United States in December.

In 1988, functional exchanges included a team of U.S. Air Force medical doctors lecturing at Chinese hospitals, the visit of two PLA National Defense University (NDU) faculty members to the U.S. National Defense University, and two PLA NDU researchers beginning a six month stay at the NDU in Washington.

MILITARY TECHNOLOGY COOPERATION

Until the Bush administration decision to suspend military hardware sale to China following the tragic events of June 3-6, 1989, munitions list items were delivered to China either on a direct commercial basis by U.S. defense contractors who possess a valid munitions license, or on a government-to-government basis through foreign military sales (FMS) channels. Equipment purchased from the United States through commercial channels so far has included S-70C helicopters, LM2500 gas turbine engines for naval ships, coastal defense radars, and communications equipment.

When the United States and China reopened discussions on munitions list arms sales and technology transfer during Secretary Weinberger's visit to China in September 1983, the official parties to the discussion were the U.S. Department of Defense and the Chinese Ministry of Defense. Their talks concentrated on identifying and defining those military mission areas, based on Chinese defense requirements, which could appropriately afford a basis for government-to-government sales of U.S. arms and military technology. Since September 1983, all high-level discussions concerning military technology cooperation have been conducted between the U.S. Office of the Secretary of Defense, International Security Affairs (OSD/ISA) and the Chinese National Defense Science, Technology, and Industry Commission (NDSTIC).[7]

From the outset, both sides have worked to define cooperative programs that satisfy fundamental goals and objectives. The Chinese have sought to acquire production technologies and systems that will enable them to upgrade their defense industries to ensure the manufacture of weapon systems and military equipment adequate to meet current and projected threats. Only in rare instances—where the Chinese defense industry had no capability whatsoever, for example, or where current threat required an immediate enhancement of capability—did the Chinese procure complete end items only in more than very small quantities. The United States, for its part, wanted to assist China in meeting its legitimate defense requirements within limits set by existing weapons and technology transfer policies, consistent with U.S. political-military objectives in the region.

Until June 1989, four military mission areas had emerged as appropriate for U.S.-China military technology cooperation. These four areas were: antitank, artillery, air defense, and surface-ship antisubmarine (ASW) warfare. In each mission area, U.S. willingness to release specific defensive weapons or technologies was conditional upon their utility to enhance Chinese *defensive* capabilities, and on a thorough consideration of the political-military environment and the interests of other U.S. friends and allies in the region.

Numerous delegations of technical personnel to and from both countries have contributed to a series of continuing discussions on matters related to cooperation in these mission areas. At every step, U.S. proposals and responses have been fully coordinated and approved by appropriate officials of the departments of State and Defense, the Joint Chiefs of Staff, and the military services. Indeed, in each case, representatives of these departments have actively participated in the discussions. In addition to coordinating with appropriate offices and agencies of the executive branch of the government, the Department of Defense has regularly consulted with members of Congress and their staffs concerning developments in the U.S.-China military relationship in general and technology and arms sales in particular.

Reciprocal visits by Chinese and U.S. technical teams have been designed to broaden mutual understanding of China's requirements and capabilities in order to refine the goals of cooperation. Chinese technical teams have visited U.S. defense contractors and military installations that may become involved in cooperative programs. Similarly U.S. technical teams have visited China, often at the expense of the Chinese government in cases approved for FMS participation.[8]

By late summer 1985, following two years of discussions and technical visits concerning the four approved mission areas, the Chinese began to submit formal Letters of Request (LORs) for specific programs. In August that year, China submitted eight LORs pertaining to the artillery mission area. These LORs asked for technical data packages, plant layout designs, and technical assistance in setting up large-caliber artillery fuse and detonator plants. Formal notification of sale of the requested items was made to COCOM[9] and the U.S. Congress in September. Initial Letters of Offer and Acceptance (LOAs) for the program were signed in August 1986. The approximate value of the program was $30 million.

In December 1985 China submitted a LOR for a program to modernize the avionics for its F-8 interceptor. COCOM and Congress were notified of the request in March 1986, and a LOA was signed by the Chinese on October 30. The F-8, a Chinese developed, twin-engine, delta-wing, high-altitude interceptor, is designed to counter the Soviet bomber threat. Avionics modernization for the F-8 interceptor involved the integration of releasable avionics components into the aircraft by a U.S. prime defense contractor. The Grumman Corporation of Long Island, New York, was awarded a contract to act as prime contractor for this program in August 1987. The U.S. Air Force was to supervise the effort as a FMS program. The estimated value of the program was approximately $500 million. The integration effort requires about six years to complete, and the technology provided includes an airborne radar, navigation equipment, a head-up display, a mission computer, an air data computer, and a data bus. Following successful integration of the avionics package, a total of fifty F-8 aircraft could be modified by the Chinese for installation of avionics kits in China. The program was an end-item sale and did not involve co-assembly or co-production. There was no plan to transfer design or production technologies. No weapons were included in the sale.[10] In order to facilitate coordination between the PLA Air Force and the U.S. Air Force, the Chinese have established a liaison office at Wright-Patterson Air Force Base in Ohio and at the Grumman plant at Beth Page, New York.

In testimony before the Senate Foreign Relations Committee in April 1986, Rear Admiral E.B. Baker, Jr., explained that, prior to agreeing to pursue the F-8 avionics modernization program with the Chinese and deciding to submit the program to COCOM and Congress, the departments of State and Defense thoroughly reviewed all aspects of the program to ensure that it was consistent with both the U.S. policy objectives and releasability considerations. "This modest upgrade of Chinese air-defense capability contributed to China's ability to protect its sovereign air space. Moreover, by enhancing China's security against external threats, this program was in the national interest of the United States."[11]

Finally, in January 1987, following the submission to COCOM in September 1986, the Reagan administration submitted to Congress a proposal for the sale of four AN-TPQ/37 FIREFINDER artillery locating radars. Following COCOM and congressional approvals, the United States issued LOAs to China for sale of the system and for appropriate operations and maintenance training. Like all other weapon systems approved for sale to China by the U.S. Government to date, the AN/TPQ-37 was considered a defensive system. The radar enables forces in the field to locate enemy radar batteries directing fire at their positions based on the trajectories of incoming artillery rounds. PLA students underwent training on this system at Ft. Sill, Oklahoma.

Cooperative programs in the two remaining mission areas—antitank and surface-ship ASW—currently under discussion—were temporarily suspended. The focus of attention in the antitank area has been co-production of the improved TOW wire-guided antitank guided missile. In the surface-ship ASW mission area, co-production of the Mark 46 Mod-2 lightweight ASW torpedo has been the main topic of discussion. Limited financial resources available to the PLA and potential competition with indigenous development programs have contributed to Chinese indecision about these programs. Four Mark 46 Mod-2 torpedoes have been sold to China for test and evaluation, and seven Chinese students have been trained on this system at the U.S. Navy Weapons Training Center in Orlando, Florida.

FUTURE PROSPECTS FOR U.S.-CHINA MILITARY RELATIONS

The pace of activity in U.S.-China military relations had slowed somewhat by the end of 1987 as the result of several factors. In China, civilian and military leaders alike turned their attention to the Thirteenth Party Congress and subsequent preparations for the National People's Congress in April 1988. Numerous senior Chinese leaders had stepped down and been replaced by others not previously involved in the U.S.-China military relationship. As a result, the Chinese have not planned a senior military visit to the United States for 1989.

Despite the rise of contention over certain issues such as Chinese arms sales to Iran and U.S. comments about Tibet, the potential for continued growth and development of U.S.-China military relations remained good.

Nevertheless, various constraints, mainly the June 1989 events, have brought the U.S.-Chinese military relationship to a halt. But in case the interaction resumes, Beijing will continue to insist on maintaining a good measure of independence from the United States, and therefore will prefer those functional exchanges which permit it to gain useful knowledge and experience without the appearance of strategic cooperation. China's desire for improved relations with the Soviet Union and the Sino-Soviet Summit will moderate, but not dampen, Chinese enthusiasm for improved U.S.-China military ties. On the technology front, probable limits on financial resources over the next several years will restrict both the quantity and quality of military technology and equipment China will be able to purchase from the United States and other noncommunist countries.[12] For the United States, domestic political considerations and institutional barriers to the transfer of advanced technologies serve as limiting factors. Finally, and perhaps most important, Washington must manage its relationship with China with a constant view to its broader interests, and the interests of its friends and allies, in the Asia Pacific region.

FUTURE CHINESE MILITARY CAPABILITIES

No adequate assessment of the implications of U.S.-China military relations is possible without some estimate of their effects on future Chinese military capabilities. Since U.S. inputs are by no means the sole determining factor in the Chinese modernization effort, two questions must be answered. What is the most likely result of Chinese military modernization efforts through the end of the century? And how is the U.S.-China military relationship likely to affect that outcome?

Since it first articulated the Four Modernizations in 1978, the PRC has sought to improve its defense capabilities through a modernization program that ranks the military fourth in national priority behind industry, agriculture, and science and technology. Defense modernization plans are geared to the long term and heavily contingent upon the progress of Chinese economic modernization. With limited financial resources available to the PLA, primary emphasis in defense modernization has been placed on military education, training, and the restructuring of the military establishment. In the area of weapons and equipment modernization, Beijing's strategy is to acquire technologies to modernize its own defense industries rather than to acquire quantities of foreign weapons and equipment. Given the present state of the PRC defense industry and the economy, it will take considerable time for the PRC to produce modern weapons in sufficient quantities to satisfy PLA requirements.[13]

As for Beijing's purchases of foreign military technology and equipment, two serious obstacles impede the transformation of these acquisitions into actual military capabilities. First, the reduced foreign exchange reserves, coupled with the relatively low priority assigned to defense modernization, mean that China cannot afford to purchase technology and equipment in sufficient quantities to effect a near-term, across-the-board upgrade of its military capabilities. Second, because China's military industrial plant and equipment, along with its doctrine, strategy, and tactics, are in most respects distinctly outdated, China faces a major challenge in absorbing the weapons and technology it has already acquired and will acquire in the years ahead. Most observers of the Chinese military, and indeed the Chinese themselves, agree that modernizing the PLA is a complex and long-term undertaking.

Therefore, Chinese military modernization efforts through the end of this century and for some period beyond are likely to result in only modest improvements to basic military capabilities. Gradual improvements in doctrine, strategy, and tactics, along with a limited deployment of moderately advanced weapons and equipment, should enhance the defensive capabilities of China's ground, air, and naval forces, but there is nothing to suggest that China will be able to redress the serious deficiencies in logistics, mobility, and command and control which at present severely restrict its ability to project military power beyond its borders.

In this context, U.S. arms and technology transfers to China are unlikely to have any great effect on the overall military modernization effort. Commercial and FMS sales to date have been quite small when measured against China's total requirements, and therefore, are unlikely to have much impact by themselves. Barring a dramatic change in the political-military environment in the region, U.S. military sales to China should continue to enhance the PLA's defensive capabilities without altering the military balance in the region. As to China's military capabilities vis-à-vis those of its primary adversary, the Soviet Union, it can be argued that an already considerable gap has been widening in favor of the Soviet Union. Indeed, one of the major considerations for the United States in approving military equipment and technology sales to China is the desire to prevent a further widening of that gap and a resultant destabilization of the region.

IMPLICATIONS FOR JAPAN

Any analysis of the implications of U.S.-China military relations for Japan must take into consideration two important assumptions. First, Japan is, and will remain, the United States's most important military relationship in the Pacific. This means that the United States is unlikely to do anything with China in the military arena that would jeopardize its relationship with Japan. Therefore, the United States in managing its military relationship with China will define goals and objectives and pursue policies which are not in conflict with goals and objectives crucial to its relationship with Japan.

Second, despite tensions in their own bilateral relationship, China and Japan share fundamental common interests. China's economic modernization requires foreign capital, investment, technology, export markets, and managerial expertise, and Japan is an able supplier to all these needs. Similarly, Japan's resource-poor, export-driven economy stands to benefit greatly from relations with China. The two countries are further bound by common security needs. Both Beijing and Tokyo view the Soviet Union as a serious threat. Soviet military expansion in northern and southeastern Asia, together with its support for communist governments in Vietnam and Afghanistan, is a source of great concern for Japan as well as China. Both countries also harbor long-standing territorial disputes with Moscow.

But Japan, like the United States, faces the challenge of achieving a balance between conflicting objectives in its relationship with China. In Japan's case, however, the conflicts arise not in balancing two different bilateral relationships, but in the context of Sino-Japanese relations per se. China's modernization in general and its military modernization in particular clearly present Japan with contradictions. On the one hand, Japan stands to benefit over the long term from a growing Chinese market for its high technology exports and from an increased deterrence to Soviet military expansionism. On the other hand, the Japanese are not sanguine about any expansion of China's armed forces. Indeed, the expansion of China's military capabilities provides incentive for Japan to expand its own military capabilities. In turn, the prospect of an expansion of Japan's armed forces is seen as a cause for considerable concern in Beijing.

AN EXPANDING CHINESE MARKET

The U.S. decision to establish military ties with China and to liberalize its restrictions on military technology transfer and arms sales in the 1980s, has opened a promising new market for Japan. As member of COCOM, Japan has been a direct participant in the decision making process concerning dual-use and military sales and technology transfers to China. And while Japan is constitutionally prohibited from exporting military weapons, it can and does export a wide variety of dual-use products and technologies.

Over the long term, as China moves ahead with its military-industrial modernization and expands its purchases of foreign products for military application, Japan should be able to capture a significant portion of the market and no doubt Japanese business aims to do just that. In 1986-87 Japan's overall exports to China declined. This current trend can be attributed in large measure to two factors. The first is the shortage of Chinese foreign exchange reserves, which is affecting the China trade across the board. The lack of appropriations to spend on foreign imports, compounded by a recent devaluation of China's currency, has resulted in an attempt by Beijing to reduce its trade deficit with Japan. Second, Chinese complaints that Japanese investment in China has been altogether too modest have caused serious strains in Sino-Japanese economic relations.

Nevertheless, the promise of future expansion of the market for Japan remains. China's needs are too great to permit Beijing to turn its back on Japan for very long.

DETERRENCE AGAINST SOVIET EXPANSIONISM

Approximately one-third of the Soviet Union's total military forces were deployed in the Soviet Far East and the Pacific in 1988. In addition to strategic forces, approximately 500,000 Soviet ground forces (almost 60 divisions) were deployed mostly along the Sino-Soviet border. The Soviet Pacific fleet is the largest of the Soviet navy's four fleets, with more than 80 surface combatants, 90 attack submarines, and 500 naval aircraft. The Soviet air force boasts more than 350 long range bombers and 2,000 tactical aircraft. Clearly, the Soviet Union is modernizing its military forces and developing its capabilities to project military power beyond Soviet borders. This military power is perceived as a direct threat by Japan as well as by China.[14]

To the extent that the U.S.-China military relationship serves as a deterrent to Soviet military expansion in the Pacific, it seems reasonable to conclude that Japan's interests will be served—although, to be sure, not all Japanese share this judgement. Certainly improved Chinese military capabilities can fortify the buffer to Soviet military expansion in the Pacific—so long as China remains wary of Soviet intentions. At the moment, with U.S.-Soviet relations apparently entering a new period of detente as the result of achievements in arms control, some observers are predicting a slowdown of the Soviet military build-up in the Far East. In the past, however, such detente has proven transistory, and we can expect that Soviet expansionism will remain an implied threat in the minds of Asian-Pacific security planners for some time to come.

Although, Sino-Soviet tensions have abated somewhat in recent years, it is difficult to imagine a return to the Sino-Soviet cooperation of the 1950s. Fundamental differences in outlook are likely to persist between Beijing and Moscow, and China is likely for its own selfish reasons to continue to resist the expansion of Soviet power in the region. Gorbachev's Vladivostok speech notwithstanding, the fundamental realities of Northeast Asian security still have not changed.

EXPANSION OF JAPAN'S ARMED FORCES

Over at least the past ten years, Japan has steadily expanded and improved the Japan Self-Defense Forces. As Rear Admiral Baker has stated, "Japan's defense effort has already become meaningful in the 1980s, now sixth largest in the world, second among non-nuclear powers. It will become increasingly so in the 1990s (when it will likely pass the United Kingdom, West Germany, and France to become the third largest), but only as a complement to U.S. forces in the Western Pacific. Let there be no question, U.S. forces provide the real basis for Japan's security."[15]

Increasing Chinese military capabilities can only provide additional incentive among pro-defense elements in Japan for further expansion of the SDF. China's past alliance with the Soviet Union and its support for wars of national liberation during the 1950s and 1960s, coupled with its size and proximity, continue to be cause for concern in Japan.

During the 100-year period prior to World War II, Japan, not China, was the principal threat to Asian security. Today, the Japanese are concerned that China may be strengthening its military capabilities with a view to supporting as yet undeclared objectives beyond its borders. Japan, like the United States and the rest of the Western economic community, is taking an active role in China's modernization, but, Japan is by no means persuaded that China will remain on its currently avowed course.

Hence, despite the progress over the years in Sino-Japanese relations, an undercurrent of distrust persists. The Chinese, for their part, have been quite vocal in their criticism of Japan, complaining about the poverty of Japanese investment in China's manufacturing sector, about the limited amounts of Japanese technology transferred to China, and about such political issues as the ownership of a Kyoto dormitory and the content of Japanese textbooks.[16] In addition, the Chinese have increasingly taken to commenting on the "rise of militarism" in Japan.

Huan Xiang, Director of the State Council Center of International Studies, recently commented on Japan's role as a regional power in a widely circulated Chinese foreign affairs journal. Huan suggested that certain people in Japan at present are crying out for militarism. Citing an analysis by unidentified U.S. experts on Japan, Huan noted a generational phenomenon whereby a minority of younger Japanese in the 20-30 year age group hold serious pro-militarist views.[17]

CONCLUSIONS

It has been said that Japan is a nation in search of goals for its impressive capabilities and China is a nation in search of capabilities for its impressive goals. If this summation is accurate, it suggests that as China develops its means and Japan develops its goals, each country increasingly will have to reassess its relationship with the other in order to promote mutual benefit and avoid conflict of interest. Japan has much to gain from a stronger, more secure, more prosperous China so long as such a China pursues domestic and foreign policies that promote regional peace and stability. Like the United States, Japan can best serve its own interest by offering China incentives to move in that direction. The past two decades of U.S.-China military relations, therefore, must be viewed by Japan in the context of U.S.-Japan political and economic relations. To the extent that the military relationship between the United States and China supported broader political and economic objectives on both sides, it served basic U.S. interests. To the extent that U.S. and Japanese political and economic objectives were parallel, U.S.-China military relations also served Japanese interests.

NOTES

[1] Winston Lord, "Sino-American Relations: No Time for Complacency," a speech to the National Council for U.S.-China Trade annual meeting, Washington, D.C., May 28, 1986.

[2] See testimony of Rear Admiral E.B. Baker, Jr., Director, East Asia and Pacific Affairs, before the Senate Foreign Relations Committee, Subcommittee on Asian and Pacific Affairs, April 29, 1986. The terms of reference used by Admiral Baker to describe U.S. policy on U.S.-China military relations have been used on numerous occasions by Secretaries of Defense Caspar Weinberger and Frank Carlucci, Assistant Secretary of Defense

Richard L. Armitage, and others.

[3.]The signing of the August 17, 1982, communiqué on U.S. arms sales to China paved the way for a segment of the Chinese military leadership to argue that the time was right to open the door to a U.S.-China military relationship. This development came at a time when some financial resources had been made available to the PLA to purchase foreign military technology and equipment.

[4.]The information in this paper concerning U.S. involvement in the military relationship with China from the time of Secretary Weinberger's visit is based on first-hand observation. At the time of Weinberger's 1983 visit, the author was serving as a military attache at the Defense Attache Office in the American Embassy Beijing. The author has held his current position as the Assistant for China, OSD/ISA since February 1984.

[5.]Admiral Watkins's visit to China was cut short as a result of the U.S. bombing of Libya.

[6.]Everyone who participated in the ship visit agreed it was an impressive event. Three thousand uniformed sailors disembarked from the three U.S. Navy ships and toured the city of Qingdao. Not since the late 1940s had the Chinese witnessed such a U.S. military presence. Despite the fears of some that the sight might evoke unpleasant memories, the visit was conducted in a superbly professional manner and the Chinese themselves had much praise for the event. The last U.S. Navy ship to visit China was the U.S.S. *Dixie*, (AD 14) which put in at Qingdao and Shanghai before departing in May 1949.

[7.]NDSTIC is often referred to as COSTIND, an acronym for Commission on Science, Technology, and Industry for National Defense.

[8.]The U.S. team activities referred to here are site surveys. Site surveys are routinely conducted as part of an FMS transfer program to assist in developing price and availability data to an FMS customer prior to the issuing of a Letter of Offer and Acceptance.

[9.]COCOM stands for Coordinating Committee, a body drawn from the NATO allies, minus Iceland, plus Japan. COCOM reviews the sale of all munitions list items to communist countries.

[10.]See Edward W. Ross, "U.S.-China Military Relations," in Martin

Lasater, ed., *The Two Chinas: A Contemporary View*, The Heritage Lectures, No. 55 (Washington, D.C.: Heritage Foundation, 1986), pp. 83-95.

[11.]Baker, *op. cit.*

[12.]Unclassified reports from both the Central Intelligence Agency and the Defense Intelligence Agency disclose that Chinese foreign exchange reserves fell from approximately U.S.$17 billion in 1983-84 to approximately U.S.$7-9 billion in 1986. Because military modernization now has the lowest priority among the Four Modernizations, the PLA is likely to be the first to feel the effects of such a decline, which will take the form of a reduction of funds available to purchase weapons and technology abroad.

[13.]The present-day Chinese defense industry dates from the 1950s and was established with the assistance of the Soviet Union. Following the break with the Soviet Union and during the ten years of the Cultural Revolution (1965-75), China's defense industry deteriorated. Today, the nation's military industry and technology is generally evaluated to be at least 20 years behind that of the United States.

[14.]See Rear Admiral E. B. Baker, Jr., "U.S. Military Relationships in East Asia and the Pacific: A Long View," a speech to the Asia Society Board of Directors meeting, Atlanta, Georgia, October 23, 1987.

[15.]Ibid.

[16.]For twenty years Beijing and Taipei have been contesting the ownership of the Kokaryo student dormitory in the Japanese courts. The decision of the high court in Osaka in February 1987 to award possession of the dormitory to Taiwan elicited strong denunciations from Beijing. In 1982, Japanese textbooks were rewritten to play down the brutality of the Imperial Army during World War II, and Beijing responded with vociferous protest.

[17.]"Japan's Role as a World Power," in *World Knowledge*, Beijing (February 1, 1988).

9

Modernization of China's National Defense
Pan Zhenqiang

From May to June 1985, a meeting that was to have far-reaching effects was held by the Central Military Commission (CMC) of the Communist Party of China. Of the many decisions that emerged from this larger-than-usual CMC meeting perhaps the most important was the one relative to a change in the guiding concept for army-building (a Chinese term that refers to the overall modernization and strengthening of the nation's armed forces). This decision decreed that for the next four decades at least, the military, rather than being structured in anticipation of the outbreak of "an early war, an all-out war, and a nuclear war" (the previous guiding concept), would be developed on the basis of an assumed peaceful world environment. Although the decision also mandated continuing efforts to modernize the People's Liberation Army (PLA) so as to enable China's military forces to be prepared for any future war, these efforts would be subordinate to the new focus of national attention: economic construction.

The 1985 CMC meeting is certain to be recorded as a landmark in the annals of China's national defense, for its recommendations are likely to shape the course of the PLA modernization program for several decades to come. This article provides an overview of that modernization process and evaluates its prospects.

CHINA'S PERSPECTIVE ON THE INTERNATIONAL SITUATION AND ON THE REGIONAL ENVIRONMENT

The primary factor behind China's strategic change of concept relative to army-building is its altered view of the international situation, particularly with respect to the assessed potential for an invasion of China.

For almost three decades after the founding of the People's Republic, all China lived under a perceived threat of imminent military invasion by one or both of the superpowers. Imbued with the Marxist dogma that world war is inevitable so long as imperialism and hegemonism exist, China viewed its own situation in light of a worst-case scenario and thus concentrated its defense efforts on developing the capability to cope with a large-scale war that could materialize at any time. From the 1950s through the 1970s, even though no invasion occurred, an emphasis on "threat assessment" pervaded China's strategic analysis, with only the name behind the threat changing every ten years or so. At the end of the 1970s, however, when Deng Xiaoping assumed leadership and reform began to sweep rapidly across the country, this emphasis began to weaken. Doubts as to whether a world war was really inevitable and whether China was indeed destined to confront a superpower invasion were first expressed in the inner circles of several strategic institutes. The debate that ensued was to last many years.

It was Deng Xiaoping who, in his typically straightforward manner and on the basis of a comprehensive reanalysis of the world situation, drew an end to the debate at the 1985 CMC meeting. Deng's conclusion: there is no present possibility that a world war will erupt, at least not in this century; therefore, the peoples of the world might reasonably expect to enjoy a fairly long stable period during which they can strive toward prolonged peace and at the same time work on the economic development of their own countries.

Deng's conclusion is important not only as an official declaration of China's new view of the world situation, but also in providing a theoretical basis for the shift in China's priorities. It also brings into the spotlight Deng's style of distilling truths from facts and, not incidently, contributes greatly to the release of China's strategists from the fetters of rigid ideological dogma.

It is China's current view that a number of conditions present in the world today will militate against the outbreak of a world war—or a full-scale war against China—for the next several decades.

First, the two superpowers, the only two countries now capable of unleashing a world war, have arrived at a reasonably stable balance of forces. With each having the capacity to annihilate the other, they exist in a state of mutual deterrence. So long as this balance endures, neither power dares resort to nuclear assault against the other. Moreover, ironically, even as the arms race between the Soviet Union and the United States has led both to accumulate fearful military might, it has not only weakened the world strategic positions of both powers but also undermined both domestic economies. Faced with this bitter lesson, both now recognize that over-reliance on military means can backfire, and that nuclear war can neither be fought nor won. Thus both superpowers seem to need a period of respite to adjust their policies, reevaluate the arms race, address their domestic economic and social problems, and aim at new strategic initiatives in the twenty-first century. This inclination has been reflected in the policies of both countries, especially in those of the Soviet Union as enunciated by General Secretary Mikhail Gorbachev.

Second, the world today is in a process of transition from political bipolarity to multipolarity. As more countries gain political independence and become increasingly unwilling to accede blindly to the policies of the major powers, they develop greater economic interdependence and more flexible trade relations. For most of these striving small- and medium-sized countries peace has become a watchword, and they are prepared to appeal strongly to the Soviet Union and the United States alike to adopt practical measures of arms control and end the threat of nuclear war. What is more, they increasingly demand a voice in the arms control process. These demands constitute an important check on the policies of the superpowers that can only serve to maintain world peace.

Finally, China believes it can play a unique role in maintaining stability and peace in the world. As long as China persists in its independent foreign policy of peace in tripartite relations among China, the Soviet Union, and the United States, it plays a role in keeping the balance between the superpowers; and as long as China maintains friendly relations with Japan, there is even greater hope that balance will be maintained.

It should be pointed out, however, that China does not regard the world situation with blind optimism. Indeed, China has a certain sense of disquiet as it looks to the 1990s and beyond. In the statements of the Chinese leaders as well as in essays in Chinese journals, it is easy to discern great concern about the evolution of the world situation over the long term. These observers have repeatedly pointed out that the new detente between the superpowers by no means signals an end to their rivalry, that confronta-tion will remain a basic element in their relations. China also notes with concern that, despite the Treaty on the Elimination of Intermediate- and Shorter-Range Missiles (the so-called INF treaty of December 1987), a new and seemingly irreversible type of arms race has already begun—this time involving outer space.

Another of China's worries turns on the rapid development of technology around the world and its potential to add impetus to the arms race. The consequences of such a new impetus are hard to predict. It seems likely that both superpowers could achieve a quantum leap in military force by the beginning of the next century, thus enlarging the gap between themselves and China. It also seems likely that some medium-sized powers will advance sufficiently to become participants in the arms race and thereby affect various regional strategic contexts.

In addition to more global concerns, China is casting an uneasy eye on its periphery, the Asian-Pacific region, where intensifying contention between the Soviet Union and the United States is disturbing the tranquility of late, and where throughout history China has been involved in border and maritime rights disputes with various neighboring states. The possibility of an outbreak of border conflicts, or even a local war involving China, cannot be totally ruled out.

Of greatest concern to China now and in the near future, however, is the specter of direct military pressure from the Soviet Union. The Soviet Union's massive military build-up along the Sino-Soviet border, its 1960s', 1970s', and 1980s' armed occupation of Afghanistan, and its support for Vietnam in the invasion of Kampuchea combine to suggest a de facto strategic encirclement of China from north, west, and south. Even if the two countries resume normal relations in the future, it will remain as hard for China as it is for Western Europe to dismiss the notion of the Soviet Union as a potential threat. Many Chinese will still question whether the Soviets' "new thinking" represents a real departure from their past ambition to replace the United States as dominant power in the world, or merely a tactic to create a breathing spell precedent to renewed expansionist adventures. Moreover, China does not see the Soviets' heretofore unabated weapons programs, huge military expenditures, and continued strengthening of military presence in the Pacific as defensive in nature. Nor is China comfortable with Moscow's apparently massive arms sales to boost India's military buildup.

In short, China sees detente mingled with turbulence, and opportunity coexisting with challenge. Though the world may be at peace for the coming ten to fifteen years, those very years could also serve as a gestation period for ominous changes in the next century. This is China's perspective on the world today.

CHINA'S DEFENSE STRATEGY AND NATIONAL DEFENSE MODERNIZATION EFFORTS

Based on the new assessment of the international situation, China's future defense doctrine may be seen as an economy-oriented strategy for peace. Its guidelines can be summarized as follows:

1)   The Soviet Union and the United States will remain the only countries possessed of the capability to threaten the survival of China. Even so, inasmuch as the possibility of an imminent all-out war has been ruled out, China can make best use of the coming peacetime period by concentrating on developing its economy and its scientific and technological base. Only by laying a solid economic and technological foundation can China effect a step-by-step increase of its defense capabilities to a level that will enable it to cope with any future threat from the superpowers.

2)   Therefore, China will firmly pursue a modernization of its national defense congruent with the overall development of its economy. In this pursuit, China must deal with the fact that the PLA's relatively low level of modernization will make it in many ways increasingly unsuited to the requirements of modern warfare, and that this situation will obtain so long as the economic and technical lag persists. China will not, however, join the superpowers' arms race. Even if its economy achieves a high level of development, China will not seek to become a superpower or to build up massive military forces beyond its needs.

3)   Although army-building remains the core of national defense construction, new emphasis will be placed on a complementary use of economic and political/diplomatic means to ensure the country's security. Here, the priority will be to promote relaxation of international tensions, particularly to ease pressures and prevent military conflicts in the Asian-Pacific area. With regard to border disputes or maritime rights disputes, China will try to reach settlement through friendly consultation; where this proves impossible, China will likely shelve the dispute until conditions change. Only if its fundamental interests are threatened or a war is imposed

upon it, will China consider the use of force in self-defense.

4) China's pursuit of defense modernization will rely heavily on distinctively Chinese resources: that is, although foreign experience, technology, and other forms of assistance will be sought to facilitate the process, stress will be laid on self-reliance and a mobilization of present assets. China's large population, for example, is a factor certain to affect the pattern of modernization and set it apart from that of other countries. Thus, by integrating advanced technology and its own domestic strengths with the larger state objectives, China will formulate its own approach to national defense modernization uniquely tailored to China's needs.

In accord with these guidelines, it should be remembered that China's defense modernization program involves many fields of effort, and that the modernization of the PLA is only part of the defense picture, albeit the most important one. Perhaps not surprisingly, some military personnel have expressed unhappiness about the resources allocated for development of the army; indeed, the proportion of the budget allocated to military expenses decreased annually since 1978. In addition, China's military industry is being oriented on a large scale to consumer production, and many military facilities have been either opened to the public or converted outright to civilian use. The complaints, however, say less about the efficacy of current national defense policies than they do about the fact that some of the military have not yet come to terms with the strategic change in the guiding concept regarding army-building.

As to the modernization of the PLA itself, the overall objective is clear: to build a leaner, better equipped and better trained fighting force that is capable of dealing with any possible future conflict. The achievement of this objective will help to ensure the continuation of domestic economic construction and to lay the foundation for development into the next century. To this end, the author believes the following must be considered:

1. Weapons technology and equipment must be upgraded.

This is one of the most important yardsticks of modernization for any armed force. It should be noted that over the last forty years, China has laid down a solid foundation for the development of weapons technology and equipment—a fact that many Westerners either do not know or tend to ignore. For example, China has already launched nineteen satellites and mastered the recovery techniques, and assembled a strong contingent of scientists and technologists expert in weapons development. But, of course when compared with the two superpowers or certain other developed countries, China lags well behind in weapons technology and equipment. In the future, in light of the assigned national defense tasks and because of budgetary constraints, China's weapons development program must focus only on key items as determined according to the "high-low" principle (whereby sophisticated high-tech weapons and equipment are used in tandem with types that are less expensive yet optimally suited to the tasks required.) Emphasis could be placed on developing the latest technologies while at the same time limiting the actual production of weapons and equipment from those technologies.

In the field of nuclear weapons, China no doubt will continue to maintain and develop a limited strategic nuclear force until such time as the Soviet Union and the United States halt their nuclear arms race. It is the author's view that before the end of this century China will probably concentrate on the development of mobile, land-based missiles. This concentration makes sense in light of various constraining factors, such as the limited resources that will be available and the characteristics of China's terrain. Such missiles are relatively economical to produce and maintain; in addition, they are relatively invulnerable and have great deterrence value. If this course is taken, however, China might have difficulty simultaneously building up appreciable underwater nuclear forces.

With respect to conventional weapons, China could seek a two-fold objective. First, efforts could be made to upgrade those kinds of weapons and equipment most likely to play major roles in any future war of self-defense—anti-tank, air-defense, C-31, and some logistic systems for example. Second, because for the foreseeable future China's security is far more likely to be threatened by low-intensity local conflicts than by a full-fledged war, development could focus on high-performance integrated systems appropriate to the needs of the various rapid response forces now being organized. Because these troops will be trained for quick deployment to a diversity of theaters whenever conflict erupts, such systems would not necessarily require enormous numbers of weapons and equipment.

China reportedly has started a program to keep abreast of high-technology developments in the world in order to predict and prepare for the future consequences of the superpowers' arms race. Although the technologies selected for greatest attention in China will be those largely employed for civilian purposes, some of them certainly could have military application.

2.   The quality of army personnel must improve.

China has traditionally attached great importance to the human factor
in war. Mao Zedong once said: "War is a contest in subjective ability
between the commanders of the opposing armies in their struggle for
superiority and for the initiative on the basis of material conditions, such as
military force and financial resources." The rapid development of weapons
technology and resultant innovations in military doctrine, principles of
operation, and tactics, all pose a demand for increased knowledge and
capabilities among army personnel, particularly among officers.

Problems the PLA has faced in recent years include: aging cadres,
decreased ability to attract talented youth (who prefer to cast their lot with
the state's new economic development projects), and, most importantly, the
inability of officers at various levels to meet the requirements of modern
warfare.

A number of measures have been taken to address these problems.
The 1985 CMC meeting handed down decisions to reduce the armed forces
by one million people and to reorganize the PLA in such a way as to
rejuvenate the leadership at various levels. These two decisions have since
been implemented with considerable success.   In addition, thanks to
preferential measures adopted by various local governments for enlisted
youth and their families, and the introduction of a training system aimed at
raising the capabilities of the soldiers for both military and civilian work, a
continuous supply of quality manpower seems assured.

In the effort to improve the competence of army personnel, formal
education has received high priority. In the past, the PLA trained its officers
and soldiers mainly by the practice of war. In the future, however, training
emphasis will shift to military schools. The CMC decided in 1985 that
military school would be a prerequisite for promotion to the officer ranks.
To implement this decision, the military education system was reorganized
to provide training at three levels. At the first level are schools that train
platoon leaders for the three branches of the armed services. The second
level consists of the command colleges for each of the services, which
prepare officers up to the rank of regimental commander. At the third and
senior level is the National Defense University, established in 1986, which
operates directly under the CMC. Its primary task is to cultivate military,

political, and logistic commanders at the corps level or above; and to provide training for senior staff of the military commands, for senior military researchers, and for high-ranking civilian officials whose work is security related. Obviously, these military schools are intended to play a central role in China's efforts to educate and train the "backbone" of the PLA.

3.   China should continue to devise innovative military strategies and tactics.

The nation's abundant wealth of military doctrines—from Sunzi on the *Art of War* to Mao Zedong's *Thoughts on the People's War*—bespeaks a tradition of, as well as an inclination to, the study and application of military thinking. Ever since its founding, the PLA has been called upon to confront enemies possessed of far superior weapons and equipment. It was Mao's *Thoughts on the People's War* and a series of his tactics that led the PLA to victory time after time over a long course of hard struggle.

Many Western analysts find Mao's thoughts difficult to understand and so suggest that their role in PLA victories has been exaggerated. In response to this skepticism, two points should be stressed. First, Mao Zedong's *Thoughts on the People's War* is the result of many years' experience in an inferior but victorious army. Second, the thoughts expressed are deeply rooted in China's soil and are the product of successful adaption to practical conditions. Thus, although Mao's thoughts might not appear useful in other countries, they have proved a powerful ideological weapon in China and will continue in some measure to apply in any future war against an enemy with superior military strength. On the other hand, it is to be expected that with the passage of time and the changing status of the PLA (from a rebel army to a state-run machine), some of Mao's thoughts might become obsolete and others might need development or revision. Indeed, this process of development and revision could well become an important task for the national defense modernization program.

4.   China should strengthen its regularization of the armed forces.

Because the PLA concentrated its efforts for so long on preparing for all-out war, regularization was not a priority concern before the 1985 decision. As a result, the PLA today looks even more like an army without a government behind it than it did before the Republic was set up. The Party still leads and runs the army, while the State Council (the Chinese government) behaves as though military affairs were quite beyond its mandate and its Ministry of National Defense serves little practical function. The result has been a rift in relations between the civilian and military sectors in China. If this rift continues, it will inevitably hamper integration of the modernization program into the context of state construction.

The command system in the PLA also manifests some traditional or, more precisely, anachronistic characteristics carried over from the days when the PLA was essentially an infantry. Moreover, the lengthy official preoccupation with the threat of a land invasion by the superpowers helped consolidate a certain measure of army dominance within the PLA, contributing to an imbalance among the services that has had a negative impact on their synchronous development. If unresolved, these problems could become obstacles to the regularization process. Indeed, regularization cannot progress unless the structure of the defense system—including the command system of the PLA—is improved.

EXTERNAL FACTORS THAT CAN INFLUENCE CHINA'S NATIONAL DEFENSE MODERNIZATION

China's defense modernization program cannot be viewed separately from the sweeping reform now in progress across the country. There is reason to believe, therefore, that despite limited resources, China will achieve its moderate national defense modernization objectives if the reform is successful and the economy develops as planned. On the other hand, certain external factors could influence the rate at which defense modernization goes forward, the extent to which it is carried out, and even its priority status vis-à-vis other national goals.

The first such factor is the arms race between the superpowers as it manifests in the Asian-Pacific region. This is a matter of great concern to China. If the superpowers keep increasing their naval and air forces and adding to their stockpiles of airborne or ship-based nuclear warheads (and particularly if the Soviet Union continues to strengthen the deployment of sea power in the South China Sea), China might be forced at some point to adopt some offsetting measures.

Second, the situation in the Asian-Pacific region could be greatly affected by the extent to which Japan transforms its impressive economic power into military power, and by the roles it elects to play in strengthening its own security as well as taking over part of the U.S. defense burden. If Japan signals that it will become a major military power or even that it will revive its militarist ambitions, China will be forced to change its state construction priorities. In that case, expansion of the navy could be given priority.

Third, a proliferation of nuclear weapons in South Asia could place China in a new nuclear framework. Such a situation would not change China's policy of not being the first to use nuclear weapons, but it might give impetus to its nuclear development program or even effect the structure of its nuclear forces. In this instance, the incentive would be great for China to consider developing tactical weapons.

Finally, there is the Taiwan issue. Although obviously China will try hard to effect a peaceful reunification of its two torn parts, its leadership in this instance has never ruled out the use of military force in an extreme situation. Should it become evident that Taiwan is intent on a complete split from the mainland, for example, China will resort to military action to head it off, no matter what the price.

It should be encouraging to us all that none of these situations is likely to emerge in a worst-case scenario. Precisely to prevent such an eventually, China would make concerted efforts in all instances to ease international tensions and to maintain peace and stability in the Asian-Pacific area, always with the goal of keeping on course with its modernization program and its economic development.

10

The Global Influence of Japanese Defense Efforts
James E. Auer

According to American critics of Japan's defense efforts, Japan is playing the United States for a "free ride," spending barely 1 percent of gross national product (GNP) for defense while the United States spends more than 6 percent. Some critics further charge that the U.S.-Japan Treaty of Mutual Cooperation and Security (MST) is one-sidedly in Japan's favor; that is, while the United States is obligated to come to Japan's assistance, Japan bears no reciprocal obligation to assist in America's defense.

On the Japanese side, critics tend to portray U.S.-Japan defense relations as primarily a series of U.S. demands for concessions from Japan. Some of these critics urge the Japanese government to resist American pressures lest Japan become needlessly involved in U.S. global strategy and thereby endanger a fragile and vulnerable nation which ought more reasonably to try to live peacefully with all nations.

What these critics on both sides of the Pacific fail to appreciate is that increasing regional and even global American-Japanese defense cooperation is in the best interest of both of these dynamic democracies. For these two economies, the two largest in the history of the world, are both dependent for their well being on free and open markets, especially in the Pacific Basin.

Particularly misunderstood by Americans, and even by many Japanese, is the degree to which Japan's self-defense roles and capabilities have become significant to overall Pacific security and in fact to global deterrence. This paper analyzes ten milestones in the globalization of Japan's defense efforts, eight of which have occurred in the past decade and owe a great deal to the Reagan and Nakasone administrations for the speed with which they were achieved. Although the effects of these developments are likely to be long lasting, it should be stressed that they do not signify any militaristic or unconstitutional intent on the part of past or present Japanese governments, nor is any such intent implied for the future. On the contrary, owing to the wisdom, vitality, and enhanced maturity of the U.S.-Japan security relationship, Japan is making an increasingly valuable contribution within the legitimate confines of self-defense.

TEN MILESTONES TOWARD JAPAN'S DEFENSE

1.   The 1960 U.S.-Japan Treaty of Mutual Cooperation and Security(MST)

When the 1952 United States-Japan Security Treaty was revised in 1960 and renamed the Treaty of Mutual Cooperation and Security, it in fact initiated a completely new security arrangement. The earlier security treaty had brought about the end of the U.S.-dominated allied occupation of Japan. Without that treaty the occupation would have continued for some additional time; under the treaty, the United States assumed responsibilities for Japan's defense and retained virtually unlimited rights to use U.S. bases in Japan for whatever purpose the United States might desire. It was neither in form nor in practice a "mutual" security arrangement, although it allowed for Japan's maintenance of the National Safety Forces, which became the Self-Defense Forces (SDF) in 1954. As a result of Japan's entry into the MST in 1960, following riots that came close to toppling the government of Nobosuke Kishi[1], the U.S.-Japan defense relationship was significantly changed.

The change was not generally recognized immediately owing to at least three factors prevailing at the time: (1) the relative strength of U.S. military power in the Pacific; (2) the relative weakness of Soviet military power in its Far Eastern provinces and of its Pacific fleet; and (3) the overall lack of capability in Japan's SDF. In fact, however, the MST formally called for actions by both the United States *and* Japan in case of an attack on the territories under the administration of Japan (Article V), but in a format differing from other U.S. multilateral and bilateral treaties owing to Japan's Constitution, which prohibits actions not in Japan's own self-defense. Further, although the MST granted the United States bases rights, these were qualified for use in the defense of Japan or in preserving the peace and security of the Far East (Article VI). The MST further specified that major changes in the composition of U.S. forces in Japan (USFJ) and their use to stage combat operations outside Japanese territory could be undertaken only after consultation with the Government of Japan (GOJ).

Most important, the MST was an independent act undertaken by the GOJ and of Japanese people who, despite tumultuous protest, accepted the treaty as an instrument in the best interests of Japan, an acceptance that has won ever increasing majority support since 1960. If Japan is indeed endangered by U.S. global strategy, as some Japanese critics presently maintain, it should be remembered that the GOJ and the Japanese public agreed to commence that "entrapment" when they agreed to the MST. Had they not done so, the Americans would not have reoccupied Japan. They would have gone home; they would have gone reluctantly, but would have gone.

2. The 1976 National Defense Program Outline (NDPO)

Although some commentators still speculate on the consequences of a "future" Japanese decision to rearm, by which they apparently mean a decision to pursue a major autonomous military buildup, in actuality, Japan began rearming in July 1950 in response to the order of General Douglas MacArthur to form the 75,000-man National Police Reserve, the forerunner of the Ground Self-Defense Force (GSDF), following the North Korean invasion of the Republic of Korea in June.[2] From 1958 to 1976, the SDF was intended to increase in size in accordance with four Defense Buildup Programs (DBPs); however, the goals of the fourth DBP were gutted by inflation touched off by a rapid increase in the price of oil.

The National Defense Program Outline (NDPO), adopted in 1976, replaces the DBPs and gives definition to the missions Japan is to assume along with the United States under the MST. The NDPO calls for Japan to be capable of dealing on its own with a limited, small-scale invasion, and to cooperate with the United States in countering a greater attack. In the case of a nuclear threat, the NDPO specifies exclusive reliance on U.S. deterrent capability.

Attached to the NDPO is an annex listing the number of basic organizational units (e.g., ground divisions, naval flotillas, and aircraft squadrons) and the main items of equipment the SDF should maintain in order to mount an effective self-defense against limited and small-scale aggression. Although the terms specified in the annex are not scheduled to be fully met until 1990, the NDPO gives more precision than previously existed to the raison d'étre of Japan's defense efforts.

3.   The 1978 U.S.-Japan Guidelines for Defense Cooperation

Japan was dealt a number of shocks by the United States in the 1970s, beginning with the U.S. failure to notify Japan before Henry Kissinger's 1971 visit to China. Later, in 1977, although Japan welcomed the end of U.S. involvement in Vietnam, its leaders did not want a reduction of U.S. Pacific forces in the face of increasing Soviet power in the area, and thus they were again shocked when the United States announced a substantial pullout of U.S. troops from Korea. This decision, too, came without prior consultation, although the Japanese had actively sought closer defense discussions with the U.S. With the signing of the U.S.-Japan Guidelines for Defense Cooperation in 1978, however, joint military planning studies between the USFJ and the JSDF were legitimized. The Guidelines have resulted in much more frequent joint military exercises and intelligence exchanges, which have produced a synergistic expansion of U.S. and Japanese defense capability in the Western Pacific area.

4.   The 1981 Reagan-Suzuki Communique

Although the Carter Administration cancelled the withdrawal of U.S. forces from Korea and announced that further reductions in U.S. Pacific forces would cease, there were no actual increases in these forces—not even in the wake of the 1979 Soviet invasion of Afghanistan, which stunned Americans and Japanese alike. Instead, President Carter's Defense Secretary Harold Brown said that, owing to the fundamental change in the international environment wrought by the Afghanistan situation, "steady and significant increases" in Japan's defense efforts were appropriate. When Japan's 1981 defense spending increase turned out to be several percentage points less than the United States had hoped, Secretary Brown (uncharacteristically for himself as well as for an incumbent U.S. Administration) publicly denounced Japan's lack of action as "complacent, unjustified, and falling seriously short." He sounded every bit as outraged as those U.S. Congressmen who had been complaining of Japan's "free ride" for well over a decade.[3]

The next month, in January 1981, Secretary of State (designate) Alexander Haig stated that the new Reagan Administration would not criticize its allies in public, but would instead pursue a frank dialogue in private concerning roles and missions rather than dwell upon the domestically sensitive issues of percentage-of-budget increases or percentage-of-GNP expenditures. On March 4, 1981, the new Secretary of Defense, Caspar

Weinberger, told the Senate Armed Services Committee that a rational division of labor among Japan, the United States and the North Atlantic Treaty Organization (NATO) allies would be a central thrust of the new administration's defense policy.

When President Ronald Reagan and Prime Minister Zenko Suzuki met in May 1981, defense was a major issue at the head of state level. In their joint communique, the two leaders acknowledged, for the first time in the history of U.S.-Japan relations, the appropriateness of a rational division of labor for defense. The Reagan Administration welcomed Prime Minister Suzuki's press conference statement the next day that Japan could, "within the framework of the Constitution," protect its territory, and its air and sea lanes of communication (SLOC) to a range of 1000 miles, and would do so as a matter of national policy.[4] This statement was strategically significant, indicating as it did a Japanese self-defense role in much of the Northwest Pacific. The roles outlined by Suzuki were easier to understand than those set forth by the NDPO, and the GOJ officially stated that the Prime Minister's announcement was not a new policy declaration but rather a clarification of Japan's legitimate self-defense roles. Both the U.S. Administration and Congress encouraged Japan to meet the stated defense goals as quickly as possible; Secretary Weinberger strongly urged that they be met within the decade.

5.   The 1983 Japanese Cabinet Decision on Defense Technology Transfer

In June 1981, one month after the Reagan-Suzuki joint communique, Defense Secretary Weinberger met his Japanese counterpart, Minister of State for Defense Joji Omura, and asked whether Japan could find a legal way for its private industry to participate in joint projects with U.S. firms as a part of the overall division of roles.

Weinberger of course was aware that, owing to 1967 and 1976 Cabinet policy decisions, Japan was proscribed from exporting arms or military technology to any foreign country.[5] However, he urged, the United States and Japan, as democracies, both have limited defense funds available, and, as allies, they have mutual needs. Since Japan is obviously developing militarily relevant technological capability, the United States has an interest in making technology flow a two-way street.

Minister Omura reported Secretary Weinberger's request to Prime Minister Suzuki, but the issue was still unresolved when Yasuhiro Nakasone became Prime Minister in November 1982. As the first major defense-related decision of his premiership, Nakasone decided that Japan's treaty with the United States was a reciprocal, international obligation that should take precedence over a domestic policy decision. By a Cabinet statement of January 1983, the Japanese Government decided to permit the transfer of military technology to the United States alone, on a case-by-case basis, in accord with the framework of the MST.[6]

The ban on the transfer of technology applies only to a very tightly defined category of "military technologies" specified in 1976.[7] Examples of banned technology are war ships, guns, rockets, ammunition, etc., that is, anything that explodes and/or does not have a civilian use. Anything that does have a civil application, even if it can be used for military purposes as well, is deemed to be "dual use" technology and theoretically free for transfer.

Japan does not have a large reserve of "military technologies" as specified in the 1976 policy because Japan Defense Agency (JDA) requirements are limited and, in view of the no-export policy, economies of scale have dictated direct purchase of equipment procured in small numbers (e.g., 12 E-2C early-warning aircraft) and production in Japan under foreign, usually U.S., license of equipment ordered in greater numbers (e.g., 200 F-15 fighter aircraft).

What Japan does have, however, is expertise in areas such as miniaturization, quieting, and precision movement, all of which have been developed for the civilian sector of the economy. In this age of thermonuclear weapons, it is hard to imagine how weapons more destructive than those already existing can be manufactured; nevertheless, the technology that can make weapons smaller, quieter, and more accurate is distinctly relevant to modern military capability.[8] Like it or not—and most Japanese almost certainly do not like it—much of Japan's civil or dual-use technology has today, and likely will have for the foreseeable future, great military relevance.

6.   The 1983 Statement at Williamsburg

The support of former Prime Minister and LDP kingpin Kakuei Tanaka allowed Prime Minister Nakasone to gain office after Prime Minister Suzuki surprised the Japanese public with his decision not to seek a second two-year term in 1982. The new Japanese leader clearly understood the meaning of the 1981 communique, and he immediately pursued a general strengthening of U.S.-Japanese ties. He and President Reagan became "Yasu" and "Ron" to each other, and already substantial defense ties became stronger.

During his January 1983 visit to Washington, Nakasone surprised some of his countrymen by stating that the United States and Japan share a "common destiny." In addition, he incurred Soviet wrath and won American attention when he told *Washington Post* reporters the Japanese archipelago is an "unsinkable aircraft carrier."[9] In meetings with President Reagan, he reiterated the agreement of the 1981 communique on a division of defense responsibilities and referred to Japan's potential deterrent leverage if an effective blockade of the straits leading from the Sea of Japan could be maintained. Upon his return to Tokyo, the Prime Minister said he had used the controversial phrases in Washington to demonstrate his determination to "defend Japan with enthusiasm and responsibility, mindful of the Security Treaty." He added that there must be "100 percent implementation of the treaty in the event of national emergencies."[10] Such phrases might not sound strange coming from a U.S. President or from another NATO head of state, but Japanese leaders who preceded Prime Minister Nakasone had usually emphasized what Japan could *not* do, even in cooperation with the United States, rather than calling for a meaningful Japanese defense role.

Four months later, at the Williamsburg summit conference, the Japanese leader held talks with West German Chancellor Helmut Kohl regarding Pershing II missile deployments, and with British Prime Minister Margaret Thatcher on INF negotiations. Thereafter, Japanese public and foreign Japanologists alike were surprised to learn that Japan had signed the Williamsburg joint communique, which opened with the statement, "It is our first duty to defend freedom and justice on which our democracies are based. To this end, we shall maintain sufficient military strength to deter any attack, to counter any threat and ensure the peace."[11] Some Japanese took this as a sign that Nakasone had abandoned individual self-defense for collective security and was advocating Japan's entry into NATO. In fact, he had not gone that far, but it was obvious that a change had occurred at least in Japan's rhetoric, if not in its policy.

Also at Williamsburg, Prime Minister Nakasone again signalled his willingness to take bold action. One Reagan White House official characterized the meeting as "the political baptism of the Pacific Basin."

126   James E. Auer

Commentator Richard Nations wrote:

However historians record the outcome of the June economic
summit in Williamsburg, United States President Ronald
Reagan's plans for the summit to "revitalize the Western
alliance" turned on a Japanese wheel. It was Japanese Prime
Minister Yasuhiro Nakasone who persuaded French President
Francois Mitterand to endorse a firm statement on arms
control and new global round of the General Agreement on
Tariffs and Trade (GATT)—Williamsburg's two major achievements, in Reagan's view. If Japan stands firm by Western
unity and open markets, who will dare to be left out?[12]

**7.   The 1985 Adoption of the 1986-1990 Defense Program as Government
Policy**

The task of obtaining the defense capability necessary to carry out
strategically significant Japanese defense goals has proved difficult, even for
the enthusiastic Nakasone. Although public aversion to anything related to
the military has diminished somewhat in Japan since the end of World War
II, pacificism is still considered a respectable position. The major opposition
to those in power, the Japan Socialist Party (JSP) and the Japan Communist
Party (JCP), consistently try to paint themselves as the guardians of the
Constitution and have long used defense as a major focus for criticism of the
GOJ and the LDP.

The one percent of GNP limit which so long shackled Japanese defense
expenditures is not, of course, constitutionally decreed. Nevertheless, it
found such public favor that neither the LDP as a whole nor any prime
minister had yet seen fit to call for its for its abolition. In his defense
budgets for 1983-1985, the best Prime Minister Nakasone could do was to
keep average defense spending in excess of 5 percent annual real
growth—but still under 1 percent of GNP—while he cut spending for most
other sectors. Even such publicly popular ministries as welfare, education,
and public works, which in most previous years had grown faster than
defense, were maintained close to zero nominal and negative real growth.

In 1985, the Japan Defense Agency completed its Mid-Term Defense

Estimate (MTDE) for the period 1986-1990. This MTDE proposes significant improvements for the three branches of the JSDF. Neither of the two previous MTDE, for 1980-1984 and for 1983-1987, had been designed to require expenditures greater than 1 percent of GNP[13]; moreover, the annual budgets, which had to be approved by the Diet and, more importantly, by the powerful Ministry of Finance (MOF), enabled only an average 60-percent completion rate for the defense items called for by these MTDEs. (The MTDEs were sometimes called JDA "wish lists"; some called them simply "beautiful dreams.")

The 1986-1990 MTDE includes weapons that extend Japan's defense capability farther offshore in accord with Nakasone's concept of a stand-off ocean defense of the archipelago. It also considerably increases spending for support items such as missiles, torpedoes, and other kinds of ammunition, which had been a critical weakness of JSDF force structure.

To extend the air defense capability around the Japanese main islands, the 1986-1990 MTDE calls for:

· increasing the number of front-line F-15 fighter interceptors, the most modern aircraft flown by the U.S. Air Force, to 200;

· modernizing the approximately 100 F-4 "Phantom" interceptors, thereby providing Japan with a total of 300 capable, tactical fighters (200 F-15s plus 100 F-4s), or about the number the U.S. Air Force has defending the continental United States;

· research on the acquisition of tanker aircraft to increase the effectiveness of the 400 interceptors and air-to-surface fighters Japan will have in the 1990s;

· replacement of surface-to-air "Nike-J" missiles with the U.S. Army's modern "Patriot" system;

· research on an extremely long-range Over the Horizon Radar (OTHR) system capable of early detection of aircraft operating in a broad area of Soviet Far Eastern air space; and

· acquisition of additional short-range, early-warning aircraft capable of detecting low-flying aircraft such as the Soviet MIG-25 that landed in Hokkaido without detection in 1976.

Sea defense, including the protection of SLOC, is to be extended by:

· increasing the number of destroyer-type surface ships from 50 to 60, or almost three times as many as are presently part of the U.S. Seventh Fleet (which has responsibilities for the entire Western Pacific and Indian Oceans);

· acquiring two guided missile destroyer-type ships equipped with the U.S. Navy's state-of-the art "Aegis" air defense system;

· doubling the number of modern U.S. Navy P-3C antisubmarine warfare (ASW) aircraft, bringing the total to 100, about four times as many as the U.S. has in the Seventh Fleet.

Capability to counter an invasion, the principal responsibility of the GSDF, is to be strengthened as well by the acquisition of modern, new domestically designed tanks, the latest U.S. Army antitank helicopters, and other associated equipment. To add realism to the capability, front-line ground units are to be redeployed and ammunition concentrated in Hokkaido and, notably, the punch of the GSDF will be extended by the acquisition of surface-to-surface missiles (domestically designed SSM-1s) capable of destroying invading forces at sea.[14]

The 1986-1990 MTDE not only finally meets the force levels called for in the annex to the 1976 NDPO; it also represents the minimum level of capability necessary to meet the 1981 defense goals announced by Prime Minister Suzuki.[15] Like its predecessors, however, the latest MTDE had no guarantee of full funding, particularly since the JDA had estimated it would necessitate an average annual defense expenditure in excess of 1 percent of GNP. In September 1985, Prime Minister Nakasone tried to gain the support of the LDP and his own cabinet to change the 1976 policy decision of the cabinet led by Takeo Miki which had set the 1-percent limit "for the time being."[16] Nakasone failed in his attempt although both an *ad hoc* commission on national security asked to look at national security policy and a defense subcommittee of the LDP had come out in the favor of eliminating the arbitrary limit. But at least Nakasone's shared interest with JDA was not to be totally denied. The decision on the 1 percent was put off as premature on the grounds that it was not necessary to break 1 percent to achieve the requirements of the plan's first year, and the cabinet approved a change of status for the MTDE from a mere summary of JDA desires to an official defense plan backed by cabinet approval. Although annual budget requests still would require approval by the Diet, the entire cabinet, including the powerful MOF, went on record in advance as endorsing the 1986-1990 defense program. With this endorsement, JDA, which as an "agency" had always had less clout than its "ministerial" big brothers, no longer had to fight for its plans on its own.[17] And given the absolute majorities enjoyed by the LDP in both houses of the Diet, approval of a budget by the cabinet in December was more significant than approval by the Diet the following March, prior to the April commencement of the fiscal year. In December 1985, the Nakasone Cabinet approved a defense budget fully funding the first year of the 1986-1990 defense plan.

8. The 1986 Defense White paper on the Flexibility of the NDPO

In 1985 in particular, revision of the NDPO was a topic of considerable discussion in Japan. Specifically, the NDPO concept of "small-scale and limited aggression" was assailed as unrealistic and naive, with critics maintaining either that aggression would be large-scale if it occurred at all, or that at least there was no way of predicting the size of an attack on Japan. Both the Prime Minister's *ad hoc* commission and the LDP defense subcommittee, which had recommended review of the 1 percent limit, also recommended review of the NDPO.

The Defense White Paper issued in August 1986 with cabinet approval finessed the issue by stating that the annex of force levels attached to the NDPO could be amended without revising the NDPO: the cabinet and the National Security Council could amend the annex as required to deal with situational changes such as the technological capabilities of the aggressor threatening Japan.[18] Revision of the Constitution or the Security Treaty would have profound political effects inside Japan and in surrounding Asian countries. Revision of the NDPO might not be as problematic, but an option to even that revision has been provided by the 1986 White Paper stipulation that the annex can be altered.

9. The 1986 Cabinet Decision on SDI

In September 1986, Prime Minister Nakasone faced the issue of Japan's position on the Strategic Defense Initiative (SDI). The GOJ had been surprised by a 1985 invitation to Japan, along with selected other U.S. allies, to participate in SDI research. The media had speculated that the prime minister would favor participation, and certain Japanese companies clearly supported the idea. But public reaction was not altogether positive, and opposition parties and the liberal press were opposed. In September 1986 the Nakasone Cabinet issued a carefully worded statement that turned out to be the most positive political endorsement of SDI by any foreign government:

> SDI should contribute to the maintenance and strengthening of the deterrence of the West as a whole. . . . Furthermore, our participation in this research will lead to further enhancement of mutual cooperation between our two countries under the Japan-U.S. Security Treaty, and thus is conducive to the effective operation of the Japan-U.S. security system.[19]

The negotiations to implement the GOJ decision were complicated by the lack in Japan of security laws of the kind in force in the United States and many other countries. By Japanese interpretation, Japan's U.S.-authored Constitution effectively limits national secrecy in the postwar period except for special measures enacted to protect military equipment provided by the United States and for regulations covering the conduct of government employees. During the negotiations concerning Japanese SDI participation, matters were further complicated by revelations that the Toshiba Machinery Company, a subsidiary of the Toshiba Corporation, had illegally exported milling machines to the Soviet Union, and allegations that these machines had caused great damage to U.S. national security.

Finally, in June 1987, U.S. and Japanese officials signed a series of documents allowing for Japanese participation in SDI research projects. Some U.S. scientists specializing in SDI research contend that Japan has more to contribute to SDI than any other foreign country. Only time will tell how many Japanese companies, if any, will actually win SDI contracts or participate as subcontractors; however, if it is true that it was SDI that brought the Soviets back to the arms control bargaining table, it is not hard to imagine how the prospect of a U.S.-Japanese scientific collaboration in the field of strategic defense might be worrisome to the Soviets.

10.   The 1987 Cabinet Decision Regarding a New Defense Spending Guideline

JDA's budget request for the second year of the 1986-1990 defense plan was submitted to the MOF in September 1986. By early December it was clear that full funding would require spending slightly more than 1 percent of the expected GNP. Following a protracted discussion within the LDP and the cabinet, a budget fully funding the second year and equaling 1.004 percent of GNP was announced on December 30.

Having thus exceeded the 1 percent, the Nakasone Cabinet had to reconcile their decision with the 1976 Miki Cabinet decision. There were suggestions that the wording of the earlier decision should be changed to read "about 1 percent of GNP," that a new slightly higher limit such as 1.1 or 1.2 percent should be set, or that the 1986 budget should be treated as a one-time aberration. In a January 1987 decision potentially far more significant than the December 1986 decision to exceed 1 percent for 1987 by a mere .004 percent, the Cabinet replaced the 1976 decision with a new one limiting defense efforts until 1990 to 18.4 trillion yen ($141.5 billion at the rate of 130 yen to the dollar), or the amount required to accomplish the 1986-1990 defense plan fully. Further, the decision limited future defense programs solely by non-quantitative factors, such as Japan's peace-loving nature, the international situation at the time, the domestic economic and fiscal conditions.[20]

Owing to the January 1987 decision by the Nakasone Cabinet, future Japanese defense efforts can be based, at least in theory, on actual defense needs with no arbitrary barrier to their accomplishment. Many Japanese commentators have noted that those LDP factions which denied Prime Minister Nakasone his desire to abolish the 1 percent barrier in 1985 owing to fears that it would extend his term in office, agreed to the new non-quantitative barrier in 1987 so that their own leaders, as future prime ministers, would not be faced with such a politically difficult decision. One moderate LDP leader observed that Nakasone had so effectively changed the course of Japanese defense policy that any future prime minister would be able to continue on the same course with ease. On December 28, 1987, less than two months after Prime Minister Takeshita assumed office, his Cabinet approved a 1.013 percent of GNP defense budget, fully funding the third year of the 1986-1990 defense plan. At that time, according to

Japanese press reports, the negotiations between the JDA and the MOF went so smoothly that, for the first time in nine years, there was no need for last minute appeals to party leaders and to the prime minister on behalf of the defense budget.

As a result of these ten milestones, Japan's defense policy and missions have become globally meaningful, and the nation has made a quantum leap in its defense capability. To better understand the progress made, it is instructive to view Japan and the SDF in the way the Soviet Union almost certainly views them.

A line drawn due west from the northernmost tip of Hokkaido intersects the east coast of the Soviet Union at a point 300 miles north of the key Soviet naval port of Vladivostok. A similar line drawn west from the southernmost point of Okinawa Prefecture touches Taiwan. Acquisition of, and the ability to sustain the combination of high technology air-defense (200 F-15s, 100 F-4s, and Patriot missiles), ASW (60 destroyers, 100 P3Cs, and "Aegis" capability) and anti-invasion (13 GSDF divisions with Hokkaido units reinforced) network prescribed by in the 1986-1990 defense plan will give Japan a significant capability to prevent undetected Soviet access to the Pacific. In view of the present and increasing capability of smart weapons possessed by the United States, Japanese capability to provide real-time, accurate locating information on movements of Soviet Far Eastern forces has enormous potential impact on Pacific deterrence.[21] The Soviets must prioritize their military efforts in Europe and along their much disputed border with China. If they show their characteristic caution about engagement in a Pacific theater which, as a potential third front, provides considerable risk owing to a high technology Japanese picket fence protected by a U.S. nuclear umbrella, then U.S. flexibility in other regions is strengthened. Indirectly, therefore, the developing Japanese self-defense detection system has global effects by allowing the United States to be stronger in other areas, thereby increasing deterrence in those areas as well.

WHITHER U.S.-JAPAN DEFENSE COOPERATION?

In 1989, the JDA will begin formal planning for a defense program for the period 1991-1995. Thanks to the January 1987 Nakasone Cabinet decision, there will be no quantitative barrier to limit the new program. Although the completed 1986-1990 program, which the Takeshita government continues to fund fully, will provide Japan the minimum level of capability necessary to meet its defense goals, the expected level of threat from Soviet Far Eastern forces in the 1990s is such that the JDA will probably seek continued steady increases to gain a more credible capability to meet the same goals.

Thus the 1991-1995 program might well improve extended air defense capability by the acquisition of Over the Horizon Radar (OTHR), long-range air-borne-early warning aircraft (AWACS) and tanker aircraft. Badly needed air defense over the sea-lanes south and west of Japan would seem to justify acquiring a greater number of "Aegis"-type naval vessels. Anti-invasion capability could be bolstered with the Multiple Launch Rocket System (MLRS), which can fire the length of six football fields, and more stand-off missiles. Improved sustainability for all Japanese forces—for example, through increased real-time command and control interoperable with U.S. forces, hardened shelters for aircraft at vulnerable Japanese military bases, strengthened harbor defenses, and upgraded JSDF living facilities—would enhance their readiness and efficiency.

None of the kinds of improvements suggested above would change the basic roles of the SDF, but their integration into the solid base JDA will have in place and on order by 1990 would go far to ensure a first-class, high technology air defense, anti-submarine, and anti-invasion bulwark very close to the Soviet Union. Undetected Soviet aircraft or shipping access to the Pacific or to Japanese territory across the Sea of Japan would be severely complicated if not impossible. Given this Japanese capability, complement-ed by U.S. strategic and smart weapons capability, one can indeed project a favorable scenario for continued Pacific deterrence.

The 1991-1995 defense program might also contribute greatly to a reciprocal defense technology flow in the course of development of Japan's support fighter (FSX) for the 1990s. One element of the 1986-1990 defense program is the selection and early development of a replacement for the domestically developed F-1 air-to-ground fighter. Initially, the JDA announced it was considering two U.S. aircraft, one European aircraft, conversion of an existing U.S. aircraft produced in Japan under license as a fighter interceptor, and a new domestic design as potential FSX candidates.

After JDA determined that none of the foreign aircraft fully met its operational requirements and Japanese industry had the capability to develop a state-of-the-art support fighter, sentiment grew among Japanese

134   James E. Auer

industrialists and in the LDP in favor of domestic development. U.S. Defense Secretary Weinberger, still refusing to pressure Japan publicly, offered to provide full information about the candidate U.S. aircraft and to share information about U.S. experiences in cost overruns and technological risks involved in the development of modern military aircraft. He suggested that Japan consider purchasing a U.S. aircraft and adding to it any Japanese technology which the JDA evaluated as superior to that in existing craft as a more cost-effective and less risky alternative to domestic development.

Certain members of the U.S. Congress clearly did not share Weinberger's scruples about pressuring Japan. Senators and congressman as individuals and in groups wrote letters to Prime Minister Nakasone and to President Reagan, many suggesting that Japan buy off-the-shelf aircraft in the United States if solely to help redress the trade imbalance. Some of the letters were made public before they reached their addressees. U.S. defense officials feared their efforts to keep trade and defense issues separate, efforts which had been largely successful thanks to the positive defense responses that had taken place under Prime Minister Nakasone, might be derailed by a U.S. uproar if Japan should decide to design the FSX domestically.

JDA next invited the U.S. manufacturers of the two candidate U.S. aircraft to submit proposals for improved versions. In October 1987, one month before Prime Minister Nakasone left office, his two-term defense minister, Yuko Kurihara, who had expressed great professional respect for Secretary Weinberger, visited Washington and announced the JDA had decided to abandon the idea of domestic development and select a U.S. plane as the basic FSX.

The subsequent JDA decision to improve a U.S. F-16 as the FSX by adding technologies in the areas of composite materials, avionics, and radar will give JDA a capable anti-invasion aircraft in the 1990s at minimal technical and cost risk. Japanese industry is acknowledged to be ahead of U.S. industry in some of the new technologies to be incorporated into the FSX, and within the framework developed to implement the 1983 Nakasone initiative on reciprocal technology flow, this Japanese-origin technology may be requested by the United States. Moreover, any Japanese improvement of existing F-16 technology will flow back to the United States without cost. Such new or improved technologies may well prove useful not only in assisting U.S. improvements to the F-16 and other aircraft in the U.S.

arsenal, but also in reducing development costs of future U.S. aircraft.

In January 1988, U.S. Defense Secretary Frank Carlucci and Japanese Defense Minister Tsutomu Kawara met in Washington and agreed that co-development of the FSX should be the first of many U.S.-Japan co-development efforts, rather than merely an isolated instance. They vowed that, despite trade frictions between the United States and Japan in other economic sectors, the two nations' industries should consistently work together rather than in conflict in the defense sector. Former Defense Secretary, Secretary of the Air Force, and noted scientist Harold Brown, has recently spoken out on the potential value of Japanese technology to future military systems. So has the Defense Science Board, a group of senior U.S. industrial executives who advise the Secretary of Defense. Both Dr. Brown and the science board warn of the dangers entailed in ignoring that potential.[22]   Their views are echoes in the words of former secretary Weinberger: "In the age of high technology defense, there are few opportunities for deterring Soviet power more promising than combining U.S. and Japanese technological capabilities."[23]

Given the geography of the Pacific and the political conditions of Pacific Asia, Japan need not project military power to effect a global security impact. With Japan's high technology picket fence in place for 500 miles either side of Vladivostok, with the United States remaining a Pacific power and the United States and Japan meaningfully sharing defense technology, the U.S.-Japan MST, so far from being a "one-sided" agreement, in fact rivals the NATO treaty in its global significance. Indeed, given the fact that in the 1990s and even more solidly in the twenty-first century the Pacific almost certainly will become the economic center of the world, the MST may soon become more important than NATO for the United States.

In summary, U.S.-Japan defense cooperation is extremely sound in the 1990s. Japan, far from being a "free-rider" or a nation "entrapped" in U.S. global strategy, is enjoying status as an economic superpower and its defense efforts are having a profound effect, not only regionally, but worldwide. The United States and Japan are indeed the two most dynamic democracies and advanced economies in world history. If they cooperate over the next twenty-eight years as well as they have since 1960, deterrence in the Pacific will continue and the prospects for global deterrence will be enormously enhanced.

NOTES

[1.] Kishi himself in fact resigned, to be succeeded by another Liberal Democratic Party leader, Hyato Ikeda. An excellent account of the treaty ratification period is contained in George R. Packard, *Protest in Tokyo* (Princeton, N.J.: Princeton University Press, 1966).

[2.] Technically speaking, some Imperial Japanese Navy units, minesweepers and amphibious ships used in the repatriation of Japanese soldiers and citizens from the Asian mainland to Japan, were still active in 1950. The minesweepers were incorporated into the Maritime Safety Agency (coast guard) which had been created in 1947 and was expanded in 1950 when the National Police Reserve was created. The minesweeping unit was separated again in 1952 to become the Coastal Safety Force which became the Maritime Self-Defense Force in 1954. Naval activities are described in James E. Auer, *The Postwar Sea-Forces of Maritime Japan, 1945-1971* (New York: Praeger Special Studies, 1973).

[3.] The Department of Defense issued a statement in the name of Secretary Brown on December 30, 1980, following the announcement of the 1981 defense budget increase of 7.5 percent. The Defense Agency had requested a 9.7 percent increase and, with the potential for an additional sum to cover salary increases, the raise could have been as high as 11.9 percent. Several pro defense LDP Diet members who visited the Pentagon during the latter half of 1980 had told the Secretary that 9.7 percent would be Japan's minimum increase for 1981.

[4.] North American Reporting transcript, "Question and Answer Session with Prime Minister Zenko Suzuki," The National Press Club, May 1981.

[5.] The 1967 Cabinet decision prohibited arms sales to communist countries, countries under U.N. sanction or countries at war. The 1976 decision widened the prohibition to all foreign countries and prohibited the export of military technology as well as weapons.

[6.] "Chief Cabinet Secretary's Comment on Japan's Offer of Equipment and Technology to the U.S.," contained in Japan Defense Agency, *Defense of Japan 1983* (Tokyo: The Japan Times, Ltd., 1983), p. 307.

[7.] The definition of "military technology" and the relevant list of military items which cannot be exported is contained in Tab B, p. 5 of "Japanese Military Technology, Procedures for Transfers to the United States," published by the Department of Defense, Washington, D.C., February 1986.

[8.]In 1983, the Toshiba Machinery Company exported four nine-axis milling machines to the Soviet Union in violation of Japan's export control law. The machines did not qualify as "military technology" but, nonetheless, are alleged to have contributed greatly to the mass production of quiet Soviet submarine propellers.

[9.]Some Japanese interpreted "common destiny" to imply the notion of Japanese and Americans falling together in battle. The transcript of the *Washington Post*'s tape confirmed that the Prime Minister had actually said "large" aircraft carrier, and the interpreter had mistranslated, recalling a popular book with the title of *Unsinkable Aircraft Carrier*. Nakasone later said he recognized the mistranslation but decided to let it stand.

[10.]Foreign Broadcast Information Service (FBIS), "Nakasone Clarifies Position," Kyodo News Service, January 25, 1983.

[11.]"Statement at Williamsburg of Seven Summit Countries," May 29, 1983.

[12.]Richard Nations, "Pax Pacifica, the Reagasone Prosperity Plan," *Far Eastern Economic Review*, July 14, 1955, p. 55.

[13.]The MTDEs employed a so-called "rolling" system whereby in the third year of one MTDE, planning for a new MTDE was completed, and the new MTDE went into effect in what would have been the fourth year of the old plan.

[14.]Details of the 1986-1990 MTDE are contained in Japan Defense Agency, "The Mid-Term Defense Program (FY 1986-1990)," *Defense Bulletin*, published by the JDA, vol. IX, no. 1 (September 1985). A good description of the potential importance of the SSM-1 missile is contained in John F. O'Connell, "Strategic Implications of Japan's SSM-1 Cruise Missile," *Journal of Northeast Asian Studies*, Vol. VI, no. 2 (Summer 1987), pp. 53-66.

[15.]The Department of Defense provides an annual assessment of the adequacy of the 1986-1990 defense plan to meet the 1981 defense goals. See Caspar W. Weinberger, "Allied Contributions to the Common Defense, A Report to the United States Congress," March 1986, March 1987. The March 1988 report in draft contains the same evaluation that the plan will meet the required minimum if it is continued on the road to full funding.

[16.]Contrary to reports occasionally seen in the United States and elsewhere outside Japan, the budget had exceeded 1 percent in the past and indeed did not fall below 1 percent until 1967. Defense spending had actually increased every year in JDA's history, but the percentage of GNP fell during Japan's years of double digit GNP growth in the 1960s and 1970s.

[17.]In effect, the 1985 decision was a reversion to the system that prevailed from 1958 to 1976 under the DBPs. From 1977 to 1979, JDA efforts were called simply "post Fourth DBP" until the MTDEs began in 1980.

[18.]Japan Defense Agency, *Defense of Japan 1986* (Tokyo: The Japan Times, Ltd.), p. 81.

[19.]Unofficial MOFA translation, "Statement by the Chief Cabinet Secretary on the SDI Research Program," September 9, 1986, pp. 1-2.

[20.]At the same time the 1987 budget was decided, it was announced that the 1986-1990 defense program would not be reviewed in the third year, as had been the case with the MTDEs, but that, as with the DBPs, the 1986-1990 defense plan would be allowed to run its full course.

[21.]For a detailed exposition of the strategy of employing precision weaponry, see U.S. Government Printing Office, "Discriminate Deterrence, Report of the Commission on Integrated Long-Term Strategy," Washington, D.C., January 1988.

[22.]Office of the Secretary of Defense for Research and Engineering, "Report of Defense Science Board Task Force on Industry-to-Industry International Armaments Cooperation, Phase II–Japan," Washington, D.C., May 1984; Harold Brown, "U.S.-Japan Relations: Technology, Economics, and Security," published by U.S.-Japan Economic Agenda, New York, 1987.

[23.]*Japan Times*, April 6, 1986, p. 4.

11

Present and Future Roles and Missions of the Japanese "Self Defense Forces"
Ryozo Kato

Over 35 years ago, William Faulkner observed: "What is wrong with the world is that it's not finished yet. It is not completed to that point where man can put his final signature to the job and say it is finished, we made it, and it works." That, indeed, will always be the case. Probably we will never be able to look at our world and say that in any aspect it is finished, we made it, and it works. Rather we will always be saying we are still working on it, we think we can make it, and we hope it will work. That qualified summation is certainly true of relations between Japan and the United States. This paper is my personal assessment of the status of current Japan-U.S. defense relations and of likely future roles and missions for each of the two countries in maintaining the security of the Pacific Basin.

Within the past two or three years the subject of U. S.-Japan trade has generated such animosity that in some political circles animosity has almost become an unofficial position. In Washington, for example, some of the voices raised remind one, in their tone if not their message, of the great Roman orator Cato who, whenever he gave a speech on whatever subject, always ended with the phrase *Carthago delenda est*, or, "Carthage must be destroyed." Fortunately, heated debate in the councils of power today is not nearly so likely to arouse a populace to violence as it was in Rome and Carthage centuries ago. However, we see around us signs of a kind of mounting hostility which remains uncomfortably close to the spirit of Cato's Rome. In the interest of moderating this spirit and clarifying its origins, one needs to touch briefly on the history of relations between Japan and the United States and make note of those developments which seem most instructive toward the nurture of a sound relationship into the twenty-first century.

Times have changed. A cliché, but in the case of Japan and the United

States it bears repeating, for here a once simple and clearly defined relationship between two countries has grown, in but a few decades, into a complex web of economic and political interests. In the mid 1960s the dominant image of Japan within the international community was that of the "copy cat" country quite without creativity but apt at imitation. Illustration of this image is the story, current about ten years ago, about the United Nations. It seems the U.N. had recruited articles on the theme of elephants from countries all over the world. The British came forward with an article entitled "The Utility of an Elephant"; France provided "Love Affairs of Elephants"; Germany supplied "Introduction to a Methodological Analysis on How to Formulate Academic Research on the Mammal Called Elephant"; and from the United States came a dissertation entitled "Market Research and the Mass Production of Elephants." Japan, however, submitted no article; instead, only a thick bibliography including all previous research ever published on the subject of elephants.

Much has changed since the time that story drew indulgent chuckles. Now there is a new environment, one in which Japan and the United States are earnest innovative competitors in the realm of advanced technology. In this particular year in which trade has been the focus of much attention, the Japanese clearly recognize not only that the United States is beset by twin record deficits but also that Japan is seen as the arch-villain behind the U.S. trade deficit. However, the rhetoric surrounding Japan-United States economic relations tends to obscure everyone's awareness of the overall progress the two countries have made.

For example, there is the issue of security, a major component of the Japan-United States relationship which is only now emerging to the forefront of debate on both sides of the Pacific, but which is certainly as equally important as the issue of bilateral trade and perhaps more so. This shift of awareness is long overdue. More than trade, Japan-U.S. mutual defense and security efforts will be the key to the preservation of peace and the promotion of democracy throughout the Pacific.

Recently in the United States, much has been made of Japan's meager efforts to provide for its own defense. Critics who level this charge often overlook one of the major accomplishments of the previous administration: a dramatic increase in Japan's security efforts. Since 1980, Japan's defense budget has increased by over five percent per year, while the general budget has hardly grown at all. This voluntary defense effort has been undertaken despite the tremendous political opposition it has engendered in Japan.

There as in the United States, no one likes to see a reduction in social and domestic programs and again as in the United States, opposition pressures set limits to the speed at which the Japanese government can proceed without risk to domestic and political stability. Nevertheless, Prime Minister Takeshita's government was clearly committed to continuing Japan's effort to enhance regional stability and Japan's self-defense. In his first budget, Takeshita called for a 5.2 percent increase in Japan's defense spending. From this and from subsequent statements of Prime Minister Tashiki Kaifu it should be clear to Americans that Japan will not abandon its defense priorities no matter who is the head of the government.

Perhaps more important for overall security relations between Japan and the United States, the Japanese government is realistic in their views toward the Soviet Union and its present leader, Mikhail Gorbachev. Although Japan generally welcomes the opportunity for greater openness with the Soviet Union, we know from over 200 years' experience in dealing with the Russians that deeds are more important than words. After Gorbachev became leader of the Soviet Union, and particularly after the INF treaty was signed, many voices were heard urging the West to have no fear about jumping on the Gorbachev bandwagon of nuclear disarmament. The hard and objective fact, however, is that despite Mr. Gorbachev's beguiling rhetoric, the Soviet intention to turn the Sea of Okhotsk (just north of Japan) into a Russian lake has not changed and has even intensified. We hold no illusions about the Soviet Union and its logic of asymmetrics—that logic which in this case deliberately ignores the difference that the United States and Japan have long relied upon their maritime powers, while the strength of the Soviet Union is and has long been its formidable ground armies. Within the parameters of this logic, the United States and Japan stand to lose much while the Soviet Union in turn loses little, if anything, by reducing ICBMs as proposed by the Soviets. This is not the case for just the Northwestern Pacific; the same is potentially true wherever the logic of asymmetrics is applied, be it in the Persian Gulf, Central America, or elsewhere in the world.

In the field of security, it is the trend that matters and not the temporary or transitional phenomenon. Just imagine how long it takes, considering all the capital, technology and material required, for a nation to acquire aircraft and missiles adequate for effective defense. It takes years. Last December, while most of the world watched a meeting between President Reagan and Soviet leader Gorbachev, Japan's air defense forces had to intercept and fire on Soviet aircraft flying with blatant disregard for

Japan's air space over Kadena Air Force Base, one of the most important U.S. Air Force bases in the entire Pacific. So far from being afraid of missing the bandwagon, Japan feels well advised to wait for another one; it may be less crowded but it may also afford a safer ride.

In the final analysis, Japan can live without the Soviet Union and the Soviet Union can live without Japan. The question then is whether both countries can find it beneficial to expand the scope of their relationship. This is a matter for cool and dry calculation. If there are uncertainties, we should wait until we are better assured of a positive outcome. At this juncture, and with all respect to the exigencies of policy formulation, one thing needs to be emphasized. For Japan, the policies of the Soviet Union are clear while ironically, the policies of the United States more often seem perplexing. To be sure, we know that sudden policy shifts are sometimes necessary as the political environment changes. But at the same time, in order for Japan to continue to develop and define its role, it is important that the U.S. government maintain a certain degree of consistency and predictability in its security policy.

Since World War II the nations of Pacific Asia have shared a great vulnerability to armed attack while enjoying much less historic and cultural affinity than the nations of Western Europe. In the Pacific region, the unfaltering presence of the United States has served as the vital linchpin holding the Asian nations together in their quest for stability and security. For these nations, as for any sovereign country, defense needs are not something which can be traded off.

Japan has the same need as any other country to build up defense capabilities to protect its own territory. In so doing, however, it must not ignore the sensibilities of the surrounding Asian countries. Japan's nearest neighbors in particular are sensitive to any hint of renewed militarization in Japan. Definitely, Japan has and should have a valuable role to play in ensuring security in the Pacific. The question is how that role is to be defined. The answer is clear and simple.

The most regionally acceptable framework for Japan's defense contribution is set forth in the present security arrangement, and the present division of roles and missions between the United States and Japan should continue. For the United States, this means a continued monopoly on offensive power projection capabilities. For Japan it means continued legal and political constraints against amassing such means of massive power projection as ICBMs, attack aircraft carriers, long-range bombers, and large land armies. Instead, Japan will concentrate on its own defense by ensuring SLOC (Sea Lines of Communication) protection for an offshore range up to 1000 nautical miles, with particular antisubmarine and antiaircraft emphasis on warfare and surveillance capabilities, none of which would translate into a massive power projection capability. Further, Japan should expand its economic and technical contribution to the common defense, both quantitatively and qualitatively.

This is not to imply that in concentrating on these relatively limited goals and missions Japan can afford to relax its efforts to enhance its own capabilities. On the contrary, to fulfill this objective Japan's defense expenditures will, of necessity, continue to increase for some time to come. This should be evident given the systems currently planned or in the process of procurement, including Over the Horizon Radar (OTHR), Aegis ships, sophisticated fighter aircrafts like the F-15, P3C, and F16, and improved early warning systems. Another area which deserves special mention is the cost sharing for U.S. armed forces based in Japan. One fact oftentimes overlooked by Japan's harsher critics in the United States is that Japan pays more in supportive cost-sharing per United States serviceman than any other American ally. Moreover, Japan's gross national support has increased significantly every year since 1979. Today Japan is spending more that U.S. $40,000 per year in support funds for every single U.S. service person stationed in Japan. These funds support personnel at over 115 bases, all of which can be counted (especially in light of recent developments) among the most stable and dependable in the entire Pacific region. Prime Minister Takeshita had committed himself to the position that by fiscal 1990, Japan will have further increased its cost-sharing budget by an additional U.S. $200 million a year.

These moves by Japan to improve its own security arrangements should not be interpreted as aggressive moves toward remilitarization. The true situation in this regard was summed up in a recent interview by Japanese Parliament member Motoo Shiina, who is one of the nation's top defense strategists:

Many people mention their fear of recurrence of militarism and a possible outward move by Japan, but you have to look at the practical realities of the situation. We haven't changed the number of our armed personnel for decades. We have only

180,000 ground troops virtually without any reserves. We have a very limited air force and navy. We have no marines. It is clear that we cannot expand our major influence beyond our shores. It is impossible. Where would they go? To China? The Chinese have nuclear weapons and over 3.5 million in their armed forces. You need a huge military force and a good sized defense industry to have a credible aggressive capability. For Japan, that would take at least ten years lead time. If we suddenly showed a desire, say, to purchase a thousand F15s, just placing an order would be recognized by anyone in the world as a potentially aggressive move and the other nations could react. Some countries could cut off our supplies. Even if we built our own defense industry, we would not have all the necessary inputs to maintain such an industry and build a full range of modern weapon systems. If potential inputs from other countries are suspended, we would be finished. Our capabilities do not reflect even the potential for an aggressive defense policy if you really look at the facts. Here our revived militarism is sheer nonsense. What we want to be sure of is that Hokkaido will not be occupied like our four northern islands. We want to ensure this by the policy of establishing a minimum defensive capability so that we can live in peace and prosper. That is all.

It is not necessary to add much to this statement. Suffice it to say that if Japan should attempt an invasion of any place in Pacific Asia, Japan would first have to expel U.S. forces.

Returning to our mutual pattern of defense spending, both countries face severe budget constraints, which are unlikely to be relaxed in the near future—another well kept secret in the United States. Because of Japan's recent trade prosperity, many Americans hold the misconception that the Japanese government has a great deal of money to spend. In reality, the Japanese government has been running a deficit as large as, and for many years larger than, that of the United States. Thus, to better the security relationship between the U.S. and Japan, much more will have to be done on both sides to more rationally allocate those defense resources available. This means an increased level of joint research and development, as well as an enhanced coordination of defense systems and material. It also means pursuing joint studies to identify the requirements for sea and land protection. Additionally, it means conducting even more frequent and consistent joint and combined military training exercises in the region.

What is more, aiming toward a more synergistic resource allocation, Japan and the United States must work together in the area of technology sharing. Many in the United States and Japan have long felt that Japan could play a larger role in providing the technology needed for today's most advanced defense systems. The recent Toshiba affair offers some clues to the host of problems potential in such an effort, and Japan has taken measures to forestall a recurrence of such problems; however, despite present difficulties, the overall trend is positive. In the last few years United States and Japanese companies have made great strides toward identifying and pursuing opportunities for the transfer of military technology. In 1987, Japan entered into an agreement to work with the United States on the Strategic Defense Initiative, and more recently the two countries have reached a major agreement on the joint development of Japan's new support fighter, the FSX.

These are the major aspects of United States-Japan security arrangements. But weapon systems alone cannot assure regional peace and stability, and for that matter regional security is little consolation to countries burdened by internal economic woes, countries whose citizens are unemployed, hungry and without shelter. While Japan must continue its defense efforts, it must also pursue non-military avenues of development by such means as increased economic and technical assistance in Asia and elsewhere. In the face of fiscal restraints in the United States and declining U.S. foreign assistance budgets, other nations, including Japan, will have not only to increase their own developmental aid abroad but also to improve their bilateral and multilateral coordination of efforts.

There are those in Japan and the United States who insist that military aid and economic aid to other nations must always be considered as a package. Objectively and realistically one has to reject that notion. It is equally important for defense spending and economic assistance to be complementary, but they must also be treated independently. Both must grow, but neither at the expense of the other. This has been Japan's policy.

In Japan, foreign economic assistance, like defense spending has received large budget increases over the last few years. In 1977, the government decided that the Official Development Assistance (ODA) budget must be doubled. Since then, that goal has been redoubled twice, first in 1981 and again in 1985. So far 98 percent of these budgetary goals have been met, so that Japan is now the world's second largest foreign aid donor (after the United States). In 1986, U.S. foreign aid totalled $9.8 billion, Japan's $5.6 billion; moreover, Japan's fiscal 1988 budget plan called for a 6.5 percent increase in foreign aid and, more significantly, a 9.8 percent increase in general grant aid. Thus, Japan is moving steadily toward greater international responsibility and is committed to increasing its efforts on the global scale.

The American people have assumed the responsibilities that go with their role as number one, or as the exceptional country in all senses, in the Free World. Over the last forty years the United States has not only enjoyed the rights, privileges, and benefits of a great power, but also, more importantly, its people have shouldered the obligations and liabilities of economic and defense leadership. The Japanese, by contrast, have yet to accept the entire field of obligations and responsibilities attendant upon their present world position.

Ambrose Bierce has defined the future as that period when our affairs prosper, our friends are true, and our happiness assured. One cannot be that sanguine concerning the future of Japan-United States relations, for in this as in all international dealings, along with opportunity come risks; along with promise, problems. The most important thing to remember in the face of such problems is that the United States and Japan, acting not only as allies but as partners, should reconfirm their mutual security interests, reinstate their roles and responsibilities, set burdens appropriate for both, and never lose sight of the fundamental desire and principles to which both countries are committed. Only in this way is it possible to safeguard the political and economic stability of the Asian Pacific area into the twenty-first century.

Janos Radvanyi was formerly a member of the Hungarian Diplomatic Service, his last post was Chief of the Hungarian Mission in Washington, D.C. Presently he is Director of the Center for International Security and Strategic Studies at Mississippi State University. For the last 18 years, he has taught East Asian and Contemporary Soviet History at the University. He has lectured widely and has written several books and articles, among which are *Delusion and Reality: Gambits, Hoaxes and Diplomatic One-Upmanship in Vietnam, Hungary and the Superpowers*, and edited and co-authored *Psychological Operations and Political Warfare in Long-Term Strategic Planning.* Dr. Radvanyi is an affiliated member of the American and International Associations for the Advancement of Slavic Studies; a member of the International Institute for Strategic Studies, London; and an Academic Associate of the Atlantic Council of the United States, Washington, D.C.

J. Stapleton Roy is the Executive Secretary, Office of the Secretary of State, U.S. Department of State. Born in Nanjing, China, of American missionary parents, Mr. Roy entered the Foreign Service in 1956. His tenure there includes a position in the Bureau of Intelligence and Research, Political Officer at the Embassy in Bangkok, Consular Officer in Hong Kong, Political Officer in Taipei, Soviet Affairs Officer in Washington, and Administrative Officer and later Political Officer in Moscow. He served in Beijing from 1978-81, first as Deputy Chief of the U.S. Liaison Office, and then as Deputy Chief of Mission when the U.S. Embassy was established in 1979 and in Thailand as Deputy Chief of Mission. Prior to joining the Bureau of East Asian and Pacific Affairs as the Deputy Assistant Secretary in October 1986, Mr. Roy served as Ambassador to Singapore.

Shinkichi Eto is Professor Emeritus, University of Tokyo, and Professor of International Relations, Aoyama Gakuin University. He has taught in the United States as a Visiting Professor at Princeton University and at the University of Hawaii. Dr. Eto has been President of Asia University since 1987. Among his numerous publications in Japanese, Dr. Eto's books include *Suzue, Gen'ichi: A Japanese Activist for the Chinese Revolution, The Political Structure of Contemporary China, International Relations,* and *A Study of East Asian Political History.* His publications in English include "Evolving Sino-Japanese Relations," *Journal of International Affairs*, 37, no. 1 (1983), 49-65; "Japanese Perceptions of National Threats," *Threats to Security in East Asia-Pacific*; and *The 1911 Chinese Revolution.*

Qian Yongnian is Director of Foreign Affairs Office, State Council, People's Republic of China. He has been with the Chinese diplomatic service since the 1950s, and served successively as a diplomat in the Chinese Embassies in Pakistan, Poland, Ethiopia, and Zambia. He served as Chief of the Southern African Division of the African Department of the Ministry of Foreign Affairs, and later became Deputy Director of the African Department. From 1985 to 1986, he was Minister-Counsellor of the Permanent Mission of the People's Republic of China to the U.N. and then he served as Minister-Counsellor of the Chinese Embassy in the United States. (from October 1986 to December 1987) Most recently, Mr. Qian has served as the Minister of the Embassy of the People's Republic of China in Washington, D.C.

Ronald Aqua is presently the Program Director of the United States-Japan Foundation, which was established in 1980 for the purpose of strengthening cooperation and understanding between the people of Japan and the United States. His areas of specialization include Japanese and Korean politics, comparative public policy and public administration, and American foreign policy (East Asia). Among Dr. Aqua's numerous papers and publications are: "The Peasant and the State in Prewar Japan," *Peasant Studies*, v, no. 1 (1976); "Japan Confronts Its Cities: Central-Local Relations in a Changing Political Context," co-authored with Michio Muramatsu, *National Resources and Urban Policy*; "Political Choice and Policy Change in Medium-Sized Japanese Cities, 1962-74," *Political Opposition and Local Politics in Japan*; "Transforming Needs into Services: The Japanese Case," *The Politics of Urban Public Services*; and *Local Institutions and Rural Development in Japan.*

Hua Di is Research Fellow, International Strategic Institute at Stanford University. His professional experience includes work as a Visiting Scholar at the School for International Studies and School of Business Administration, University of Washington in Seattle, a Research Fellow for the Northeast Asia-U.S. Forum on International Policy, Stanford University, and a Research Fellow at the East-West Center, Honolulu. In December 1986, Dr. Hua became Co-Director of CITIC Research International. In June 1989, Dr. Hua became a research fellow at the International Strategic Institute at Stanford University. Dr. Hua's published papers in English include, among others, "Chinese Comprehensive Strategic Doctrine," in *The Role of Technology in Meeting the Defense Challenge of the 1980's*, "Global Strategy and US-PRC Relations," in *Mainland China, Taiwan, and US Policy*, and "The Soviet Threat to the Northern Pacific Region from an Overall Point of View," *Atlantic Community Quarterly* (Spring 1986).

Rear Admiral Edward B. Baker, Jr., USN is currently Commander, Amphibious Group Three, San Diego, California. In 1967, he began a tour in the office of the Chief of Naval Operations, Systems Analysis Division. He has commanded the USS BRONSTEIN, USS DAVID R. RAY, and Destroyer Squadron THIRTY-THREE. He served as a Staff Assistant to the Secretary and Deputy Secretary of Defense, Head of General Purpose Forces Branch of the Systems Analysis Division of the Office of the Chief of Naval Operations, and as Executive Assistant to the Commander of U.S. Forces in the Pacific. Previously, Admiral Baker was assigned as Assistant Chief of Staff for Operations on the staff of the Commander in Chief of the U.S. Pacific Fleet and as Director, East Asia and Pacific Region, Office of Assistant Secretary of Defense, International Security Affairs.

Edward W. Ross is Special Assistant for China, Office of the Secretary of Defense, International Security Affairs, Washington, D.C. He served in Vietnam, where he commanded a detachment of the 525th Military Intelligence Group, and in Hawaii, where he commanded a detachment of the 500th Military Intelligence Group from 1973 to 1976. As a U.S. Army Foreign Area Officer specializing in Chinese Affairs, he served as a political-military China analyst in the Directorate for Estimates, Defense Intelligence Agency, and as the Assistant Army Attache to the People's Republic of China from 1983 to 1984. Mr. Ross retired from the U.S. Army as a Lt. Colonel in August, 1984. His publications include "Chinese Conflict Management," *Military Review*, (Jan. 1980); "U.S.-China Military Relations,"

The Two Chinas: A Contemporary View; and "U.S.-China Military Relations: The Implications for ASEAN," *China and ASEAN.*

Pan Zhenqiang is the Deputy Director, Institute for Strategic Studies, National Defense University, Beijing, People's Republic of China. After graduating from the University of Dr. Sun Yesan, he joined the armed forces and worked in the Army's units as well as in the General Staff for many years. Since then, he has been doing research work in various institutes of the People's Liberation Army. As a member of the Chinese delegation, he has been involved in disarmament negotiations. He is now a Senior Research Fellow at the Institute for Strategic Studies, National Defense University, People's Liberation Army, China, and a Visiting Fellow at the International Strategic Institute, Stanford University. His major field of study is international security and arms control issues.

James E. Auer is presently the Director, United States-Japan Center, at Vanderbilt University. He served in the U.S. Navy in a number of positions, largely in Japan. These included political adviser to the Commander of U.S. Naval Forces in Japan, visiting student at the Japan Maritime Self-Defense Force Staff College in Tokyo, and commanding officer of a guided missile frigate homeported in Yokosuka. Dr. Auer subsequently served as Special Assistant for Japan, Office of the Secretary of Defense. His book, *The Postwar Rearmament of Japanese Maritime Forces, 1945-1971,* was published in English by Praeger Publishers and in Japanese under the title, *Yomigaeru Nippon Kaigun.*

Ryozo Kato is a Minister (Political) in the Embassy of Japan in Washington, D.C. Mr. Kato entered Japan's Ministry of Foreign Affairs in 1965. His numerous positions in the Foreign Ministry include service in the First North American Affairs Division, North American Affairs Bureau, and in the General Affairs Division. He served as First Secretary in the Embassy of Japan in Canberra, Australia, and as First Secretary in the Embassy of Japan in Cairo, Egypt. As Director in Charge of the Summit Meeting of Seven in Ottawa, Mr. Kato was with the Economic Affairs Bureau of the Ministry of Foreign Affairs. He served as Director of the Ministry's National Security Affairs Division, North American Affairs Bureau, and as Director of the Treaties Division of the Ministry's Treaties Bureau.

Selected Bibliography

Auer, James E. *The Postwar Sea-Forces of Maritime Japan, 1945-1971*. New York: Praeger Special Studies, 1973.

Barnett, Robert W. *Beyond War: Japan's Concept of Comprehensive National Security*. New York: Pergamon-Brassey's, 1984.

Berger, Peter L., and Michael Hsiao, eds. *In Search Of An East Asian Development Model*. New Jersey: Transaction Books, 1988.

Calder, Kent. *Crisis and Compensation: Public Policy and Political Stability in Japan 1949-1986*. Princeton, New Jersey: Princeton University Press, 1988.

Christopher, Robert. *Second to None: American Companies in Japan*. New York: Crown Publishers, Inc., 1986.

Cohen, Stephen D. *Uneasy Partnership: Competition and Conflict in Contemporary U.S.-Japanese Trade Relations*. Cambridge, Massachusetts: Ballinger Publishing Company, 1984.

Emmerson, John K., and Harrison M Holland. *The Eagle and the Rising Sun: America and Japan in the Twentieth Century*. Massachusetts: Addison-Wesley, 1989.

Gilbert, Stephen P., ed. *Security in Northeast Asia: Approaching the Pacific Century*. Boulder, Colorado: Westview Press, 1988.

Gregor, James. *Arming the Dragon: US Security Ties with the Peoples*

Republic of China. Washington: Ethics and Public Policy Center, 1988.

Grinter, Lawrence and Young Whan Kihl, eds. *East Asian Conflict Zones.* New York: St. Martin's, 1987.

Hamrin, Carol Lee. *China and the Challenge of the Future; Changing Political Patterns.* San Francisco: Westview Press, 1990.

Japan Defense Agency. *Defense of Japan 1986.* Tokyo: The Japan Times Ltd., 1986.

Kallgren, Joyce K., and others eds. *ASEAN and China: an Evolving Relationship.* Berkely: Institute of East Asian Studies, University of California, 1988.

Keith, Ronald C., ed. *Energy, Security, and Economic Development in East Asia.* New York: St. Martin's Press, 1986.

Kim, Ilpyong J., ed. *The Strategic Triangle: China, the United States, and the Soviet Union.* New York: Paragon House, 1987.

Kim, Roy and Hilary Conroy, eds. *New Tides in the Pacific: Pacific Basin Cooperation and the Big Four (Japan, PRC, USA, USSR).* Westport, Connecticut: Greenwood Press, 1987.

Krauss, Willy and Wilfried Lutkenhorst. *The Economic Development of the Pacific Basin; Growth Dynamics, Trade Relations, and Emerging Cooperation.* New York: St. Martin's Press, 1986.

Lampton, David M., and Catherine H. Keyser, eds. *China's Global Presence.* Washington: American Enterprise Institute, 1988.

Morrison, Charles E. and Frances Fung Wai Lai, eds. *Political and Security Cooperation: A New Dimension in ASEAN-Japan Relations.* Japan: Komiyama Printing Co., Ltd., 1987.

Morse, Ronald A., ed. *US-Japan Relations: An Agenda for the Future.* Honolulu: Pacific Forum, 1989.

Nakamura, Takafusa. *Economic Development of Modern Japan.* Japan: Ministry of Foreign Affairs, 1985.

Ohmae, Kenichi. *Triad Power: The Coming Shape of Global Competition.* New York: The Free Press, 1985.

Packard, George R. *Protest in Tokyo.* Princeton, New Jersey: Princeton University Press, 1966.

Pyle, Kenneth B. *The Trade Crisis: How will Japan Respond?* Pennsylvania: Science Press, 1987.

Ross, Edward W. "U.S.-China Military Relations." In *The Two China's: A Contemporary View,* The Heritage Lectures, ed. Martin Lasater, 83-95. Washington, D.C.: Heritage Foundation, 1986.

Scalapino, Robert A. and others, eds. *Pacific-Asian Economic Policies and Regional Interdependence.* Berkeley: Institute of East Asian Studies, University of California, 1989.

Scalapino, Robert A. and Masataka Kosaka, eds. *Peace, Politics, and Economics in Asia.* Washington: Pergamon-Brassey's, 1988.

Simon, Sheldon. *The Future of Asian-Pacific Security Collaboration.* Massachusetts: Lexington Books, 1988.

Simon, Sheldon W. *The ASEAN States and Regional Security.* Stanford, California: Hoover Institution Press, 1982.

The Atlantic Council of the United States & The Research Institute For Peace and Security, Tokyo. *The Common Security Interests of Japan, the United States, and NATO.* Cambridge, Massachusetts: Ballinger Publishing Company, 1981.

Wolferen, Karel von. *The Enigma of Japanese Power.* New York: Knopf, 1989.